FATHERS: A FRESH START FOR THE CHRISTIAN FAMILY

FATHERS

A Fresh Start for the Christian Family

Robert R. Iatesta

SERVANT BOOKS
Ann Arbor, Michigan

Most scripture texts used in this work are from *The New American Bible* copyright © 1970 by the Confraternity of Christian Doctrine

Available from Servant Books, Box 8617, Ann Arbor, Michigan 48107

Printed in the United States of America

ISBN 0-89283-083-2

Dedication

This book is dedicated to our family:

To my wife Anna, who continues to love me in season and out; without whom this book would never have been written.

To our children, Robert, Lorraine, Michelle, John, Thomas, and Daniel who are the fruit of our life in Christ and a personal delight.

To our parents, John and Lillian Iatesta — who gave me life and always loved me, and Daniel and Mae DiBona — who gave me their daughter and lovingly welcomed me into their lives.

Acknowledgements

The fruit of this work is due primarily to the leading of the Holy Spirit, the consistent encouragement and discernment of my wife Anna, and the spiritual guidance of Most Rev. Edward T. Hughes, Auxiliary Bishop of Philadelphia, Pa.

Beside these, I would like to thank:

The many dedicated friends and relatives, especially Pete and Fran Radice, Frank and Joan DiBona, and their families for their constant affirmation and prayer.

The Reagan, Farrow, Leopold, and Bonella families for their ongoing support.

Robert and Kathleen Conway for patiently and lovingly working on raw outlines and early manuscripts.

Jack and Marilyn Craig for the hours spent with editorial review.

Jim Manney and Bert Ghezzi for their faith in me and a great job of editing.

Fr. Domenic Rossi and Abbot John Neitzel for allowing me to draw freely upon the physical and spiritual resources available at the Daylesford Abbey.

William Gannon and Fr. Richard Jones for providing the peace and quiet of the Ephphatha Community Prayer Center.

Finally, all those who helped with miscellaneous needs, especially Ed Cavallaro, Chuck Campbell, Jim Owens, Tom Brinker, Josephine Rowell, and Peg Walsh.

Contents

PROLOGUE

This book is about change. It describes the changes which have happened in our family and in others who have begun to take the gospel of Jesus seriously. This book does not deal with all aspects of the transformation which God wants for families; rather, it focuses on one member of the family: the father. The father's conversion to Jesus and his ongoing spiritual restoration are the keys to the family's life in Christ. As he changes, so does his family.

Change is one of the few things in this life which is constant, something we can expect to occur. It's a lifelong process which is used by God to draw us closer to him. As we exchange our preoccupation with physical and psychological attributes for relationships with God and others, the process of change effects the desired result—a movement back to our Father's house. Hopefully, at the end of our journey, we will rest in his arms—fully one with him.

The following events led to some critical changes in my life.

In 1965, a desire for "something more" began to grow in our family. The impact of Vatican II had just begun to take hold in the Catholic Church. Through my wife Anna's searching, we were led to a local Christian adult education class on scripture and lay spirituality. The classes were our first mutual response to the new hunger within us. It didn't take long to discover how undeveloped I was in these areas, but God had provided a beginning.

Those years were also filled with a great deal of natural change in our lives: three babies close together, a new home, my father's death, to name a few. In spite of all this, a pattern of material success continued. The real challenge for me came when our first child reached age five. This event provoked direct questions in me about my relationship with God. After my father's death, the questions got more direct—I had no answers.

1

My exposure to adult Christian education eventually led me to men and women involved in the Cursillo, a movement for renewal within the Catholic Church. Their vibrant witness prompted Anna and I to apply to attend a Cursillo weekend. We were both accepted, but schedules conflicted. After a year's wait, the time for my weekend arrived. Despite my curiosity, I approached this new situation personally protective. However, the three days of intense teaching and witness in a community setting cracked my shell, and on Sunday, the last day of the weekend, the unconditional love of God melted my heart.

Many years have passed since that spring in 1968, but the joy and the power of my conversion experience remain a vivid memory. Close friends and family recognized that a "new man" had come back from the Cursillo. Today, however, as I stand back and view my Christian initiation in perspective, I can see that the gentle, loving hand of the Father was protecting a baby in his kingdom. I had enthusiasm for God, but he wanted much more from me.

The five years that followed my weekend were almost totally dedicated to service in the Cursillo movement. However, as my business continued to flourish, the time away from home working in "my apostolate" was becoming a source of conflict for Anna and I. I spent myself in outside activities, while the Lord held things together at home. During those early years, I learned a great deal about God as my Father, Jesus as my brother, and the excitement of leading men to Christ.

After 1970, the Lord began to work a deeper change in my life. While on a retreat at a Carmelite monastery, I sensed three clear directives for my personal maturity in the Christian life: balance, simplicity, and fidelity to covenant! Although I did not understand the meaning of these words at the time, I knew God was beginning to direct me in a new way. He revealed the spiritual poverty in my children, the complexities of my life, and the untapped power and wisdom in our marriage. I sensed these words long before I was equipped or willing to act on them.

My first response was toward balance and simplification. Anna and I began to step back from various spiritual and social activities. Together we made a serious commitment to our call as Christian parents. With prayer came the realization that we had made idols of many situations and people. We slowly released areas to the Lord for change as he showed them to us. The beginnings of simplification were painful; our aloneness drove us to a new level of prayer.

Eventually we were led into the charismatic renewal and baptism in the Holy Spirit. The increased activity of the Spirit began a work of transformation in my thought patterns, motives, attitudes, and priorities. The Holy Spirit started teaching me his truth in each area of my life. The process was slow but steady.

I learned that all service for God begins in prayer. Through quiet listening came the understanding that we needed to base our lives on God's word and its practical application. Slowly a hunger developed for working knowledge of Christian family life.

This process would not have been possible without the loving support of my wife, Anna. She is totally dedicated to her call, and is finding the peace and joy of Jesus in a fuller way each day. Her "yes" to faith allowed God to change my life. Her steady encouragement was a major factor in the writing of this book.

The idea of writing was not on my mind as I stepped back from my business career in 1977 to seek out deeper service for the Lord. For about two years, there had been a growing sense that God had some major revisions in mind for us. Not understanding just what was coming, I began praying for faith and wisdom to respond when he called. The timing of the Lord is perfect; when I was ready to withdraw from my career, that was his plan for me.

The first few months were very challenging. Change is never easy. Yet, I discovered that God had been preparing me to change for a long time. After looking unenthusiastically at some good business offers, I knew something new was in store for us. Once I surrendered my ideas of just what that was, God started to move.

Within a couple of weeks, three people suggested that I write a book. A pleasant smile was my response to the first, but when the others came, I knew this suggestion might be the Lord's word to me. I went ahead, into the difficult, yet exciting experience of learning to write. Here again, the Spirit had been preparing the soil for many years. I found much of the resource material I needed in the daily prayer journal which I had been keeping for years. Good friends, willing to help, provided the rest.

Writing has given me the opportunity to look back and try to discover how the miracle of conversion and restoration happens. I believe it comes down to two important words which came from one of our children. When asked what made our life different today, he responded: *prayer and support*. We need God and others, divine and human relationships.

The thought that "no man is an island" is especially true as we grow into maturity in Christ. We need daily contact with the Lord in prayer and the encouragement, affirmation, and challenge of others who have similar values and hunger. As fathers, our deepest support should come from our wives, the partners in our marriage covenant. Although the subject of this book is the father, I want to clearly state that he is only one part of the pastoral team which God has assigned to a family. I would not have been able to serve effectively as a father, nor could our family have experienced the change it has, without Anna's total support and dedication. She has embraced her call as a wife and mother.

A few comments from Harold M. Voth, a noted psychiatrist and psychoanalyst, generally sum up my views. He says:

Mothering is probably the most important function on earth. It requires a high order of gentleness, commitment, steadiness, capacity to give, and many other qualities. A woman needs a good man by her side so she will not be distracted and depleted, thus making it possible for her to provide rich humanness to her babies and children. Her needs must be met by the man and above all she must be secure. A good man brings out the best in a woman, who can then do her best for the children. Similarly, a good woman brings out the best in a man, who can then do his best for his wife and children. Children bring out the best in their parents. All together they make a family, a place where people of great strength are shaped, who in turn make strong societies.

Adding to the natural support within the nuclear family, we have found that God has provided grandparents and Christian friends. The witness of selfless love we have seen in our parents and the consistent encouragement of our intimate friends continue to build rings of love around our family.

Beyond these first circles of love, the need is ever-present for support of the larger body: Church and faith community. These outer layers of support build up the family, giving it an identity beyond itself.

Each of these souces of love will help the family in its growth process, but we must start with *grace*—God's common denominator. Despite the task, every family in the Church has the grace for change by virtue of the marriage sacrament. Each of us, no matter what condition of incompleteness we live in, can begin to move toward the Lord and experience the peace, joy, and love he promises. Grace, God's life within us, makes this possible. The power to bring forth new life is present. All that is needed to begin the process is for one person; man, woman or child, to call upon the name of the Lord:

Our soul waits for the Lord,
Who is our help and our shield,
For in Him our hearts rejoice;
In His Holy name we trust.
May your kindness, O Lord,
Be upon us who have put our hope in you.
(Ps 33:20-22)

As I wrote this book, part of God's plan became clear to me. I believe it is part of his plan to change the focus of men's hearts from personal achievement to their primary relationships: God and their families. Spiritually renewed fathers are a key link in the Lord's promise to renew the face of the earth. Families able to live in Christ will flow from the deeper transformation of Christian men. The Church is in desperate need of families with a clear sense of priorities and an apostolic zeal. The world needs working models of grace.

Very few men are prepared for the challenges and the opportunities of marriage and family life. It is my sincere hope that this book will help fill that void. This book is directed to the deepest need in our preparation and development: our relationship with God. Only the Lord can teach a man how to become a Christian father. Only he can lead us into abundant life.

This is not a book about the techniques of being a parent, but it concerns the spiritual restoration of a man. I offer my experiences to you as evidence of *hope* that God can change a natural father into a Christian father.

At the same time, the events described in these pages are not theories; nor are they isolated experiences. They are personal experiences which I have seen duplicated in other families. The changes we've undergone are uniquely ours, but I know they are not meant just for us. The Lord wants everyone to experience new life in him. This book stems from a belief that God wants the *best* for all families and the men who are called to lead them.

Finally, this book will offer numerous suggestions to develop your fatherhood in Christ. It will provide tools to use as you cooperate with God's spirit in the development of your family.

As you begin, may I offer this word of hope and encouragement: God's way works and it is possible!

PART ONE

A Father's Identity

CHAPTER ONE

A Call and a Decision

Early one morning several years ago, I was awaiting the birth of our fourth child. Unlike the three previous deliveries, I was unusually calm in the father's room at Lankenau Hospital, just outside of Philadelphia. Despite having been up for a while, fatigue was not apparent as I sat reading my pocket New Testament. It had been about fifteen months since my "new life in Christ" began. The memory of that moment of grace was still vivid as I waited for some news about Anna and our child.

When the doctor breezed in, dressed in his operating "greens," I knew by the smile on his face that we had a fine healthy baby. "A big boy," he said. I replied, "Praise God, what a blessing," and went immediately to see our son. Looking at him, a strange sense of awe came over me. It was Pentecost Sunday, the birthday of the Church.

John's birth marked a beginning for our "domestic church" as well as an anniversary for the universal body. God the Father began to unfold a plan which is bringing restoration in Christ to our family and a new understanding of vocation. I was soon to see my call to fatherhood as much more than mere paternity.

The transformation which God wants for Christian families must begin with someone. In our case it was Anna. She made the first adult "yes" to God and began searching for his will. That drew me into my "yes." Once both of us had accepted individual conversion, the Lord continued in his way, teaching us to live as a family in Christ.

Spiritual restoration of a family has many characteristics similar to individual human development. From conception through birth, growth and adulthood, the common thread is *process*. Growing up has high and low points. There is no growth or change without experiencing both. While happiness makes life memorable, deeper learning seems to occur in our painful moments. On the anvil of adversity, character and strength are forged.

The growth process of a Christian man and his family will follow the same trends. While our initial encounter with the Lord lifts us toward faith, hope and love, continuing formation entails cycles of rapid growth mixed with diligent application of wisdom. The call to fatherhood and our response is usually the beginning of an up-cycle. God's invitation and our acceptance are the critical points.

Changed Life

Changed life in a family is tied to a changed father. It begins when he hears a call from God and responds positively with decision and action. Let me explain how this was worked out for me.

Although John's birth was peaceful, the days that followed were in turmoil. Anna began experiencing severe headaches, then high fevers; she had to be re-hospitalized a week after bringing John home. I suddenly found myself with three children under seven and a new baby to care for. Pruning and testing had begun. During those days I learned how to beg for God's mercy and pray with a sincere heart. The infection which had put Anna in bed lasted for months. Whenever it seemed like I had reached my limit of faith, another crisis would arise. Through it all, I could sense God urging me to keep going. He provided the grace needed.

Today, I recognize the fruit of those painful days. In desperate need, with my wife seriously ill and four young children to care for, my heart was opened to God wider than ever before.

When the crisis finally passed, I was a changed man. I saw that *his* grace is sufficient.

That experience taught me a lot about the needs of a family. I learned how important the roles of father and mother are, since I had to be both. Also I realized our need as a family for a deeper spiritual life. While addressing our physical situation, Anna and I learned to pray together even though she was in a hospital and I was doing housework. Despite adversity, a conviction grew that God had something more in mind for us, and that it was going to be exciting and life-giving. In the midst of crisis, the Lord placed a hunger in our hearts to experience Christ as a family. We didn't fully respond to that first invitation, yet seeds had been planted.

When Anna recovered, we quickly returned to our old patterns. For the next few years, I concentrated on my business career and Anna took care of our home. We ignored the call to deepen our relationship with God as a family, and instead went the route of many young married couples who have had some experience of personal renewal: We plunged into church activities, neglecting both our marriage and the children. Our frenzied efforts as modern-day apostles caused many others to be stirred to faith, but things didn't change very much at home. The baby-sitters were the same as before. Our children would ask sheepishly, "Are you going out again?" Those words rang in my ears as we dashed out to serve and love those "others."

We resisted hearing what our children were saying. I can vividly remember doing "holy things" on weekends and then being too tired to even wake up on Monday mornings. The kids wanted to hug and kiss their daddy, but I just wanted to pull the covers over my head. A spiritual high seemed more rewarding than the daily life of service to my family.

After a few years of "Monday morning blues," the Lord finally broke through. In prayer one morning I was led to this reading: "The king will say to those on his right: 'Come. You have my father's blessing! Inherit the kingdom prepared for you from the creation of the world. For I was hungry and you gave me food, I was thirsty and you gave me drink'"

(Mt 25:34-35). Finally the light of Christ dawned; I realized that our children were starving for visible Christian parents. They were the first poor and hungry which God wanted Anna and I to feed. If they were not emotionally and spiritually cared for, all our external ministry would be just "a noisy gong and a clanging cymbal." My heart had been prepared; now the Lord was ready to speak. This time I listened.

God brings about change in us by first stirring a hunger or need in our hearts, and then directing us to a source of wisdom which can satisfy that need. For me, the hunger to see my family renewed in faith came first. Then came a discovery that I could hardly hear God's instructions about how to satisfy this need while on the run. To be taught by the Spirit, I had to slow down and step back from many good and holy activities. The Lord was saying, "Be still, and know that I am God" (Ps 46:11). I finally came to rest.

Anna and I settled down and learned how to pray again. As we listened to God, asking for his perspective on our family, the Father's love and mercy became clear. Along with revelation of the spiritual poverty in our home came his promise of faithfulness. Gently, he showed us it was not too late to change. We could rely on his fidelity to covenant. Perseverance in prayer brought understanding of how God intended to care for us. He exposed us to knowledge of his transforming power and provided living witnesses to demonstrate it. God was going to fill our needs in a variety of ways, with different kinds of people.

One of the first models of grace he sent us were Gary and Barbara Morgan, a couple who had recently moved from Phoenix to Philadelphia. The Morgans stayed in Philadelphia for only a short while, but in that time they built our faith and hope. They didn't provide all the answers we needed, but they taught us to ask the right questions of ourselves and of God. They were the first in a series of people and events the Lord used to form us into a Christian family. Slowly we grew in hope that there was something more—a lot more.

Despite God's intervention in many wonderful ways, change came slowly. It became clear that inspirational witnesses and knowledge were not the whole answer. A major part of the process of change had eluded us. This missing step was an act of the will on the part of a key family member—the father. Growth was available but it involved something from me. The something was *decision!* I had heard the call to Christian family life, but I hadn't decided to let God change me into a Christian father.

Before we can decide for fatherhood, we should have a clear understanding of what's involved. Let's address this basic question.

What Is Christian Fatherhood?

A Christian father is a man who has heard the call to reflect God to his family and is responding to that call. He is actively cooperating with the Holy Spirit to lead and form others into the image and likeness of the Creator. He is a man who is willing to act in God's name, trusting that Jesus can accomplish his work through him. He is a father who has accepted his role as spiritual leader of his family, a man who knows his weakness and trusts God to be God.

The ideal for Christian fatherhood is contained in Jesus' description of the Fatherhood of God. Jesus taught us four important things about God: He is a Father; he is the source of all authority; he uses his power to gather persons into unity; and that three persons make up the Godhead. In short, the nature of God is *family*. "In my Father's house there are many dwelling places; otherwise, how could I have told you that I was going to prepare a place for you" (Jn 14:2). Doubting his promises, as we often do, the disciples questioned him further, "'Lord,' said Thomas, 'we do not know where you are going. How can we know the way?' Jesus told him: 'I am the way, and the truth and the life; no one comes to the Father but through me'" (Jn 14:5-6).

Jesus is telling us that he and he alone will lead us into knowledge of God and relationship with him. What's more, heaven is like a home and God is the Father of a family. The call to fatherhood necessitates a response to Jesus. He is the way to the Father. We have one father who is God and one teacher who is Jesus (Mt 23:9-10). In addition to revealing God as family, Jesus shows us that we can begin to share in the fullness of God's life right now through the ministry of the Holy Spirit. His promise is unconditional: "I came that they may have life and have it to the full" (Jn 10:10).

A Christian father believes this good news and lives it. He is called by Jesus to be a reflection, imperfect as he may be, of the Fatherhood of God.

Another way of putting it is to say that a Christian father is a man in full relationship with the Trinity. He is an obedient son of God the Father; he is a brother to Jesus, listening to the Word and following the Way. This loving contact with the Father and the Son makes a man *teachable*. He is thus able to be led by the Spirit, who teaches him the wisdom of God.

As he grows in his identity as a son of God and brother of Jesus, the Christian father is prepared for his principal mission as spiritual leader of his home. He and his wife "enspirit" the family. Their roles in this mission are distinct yet complementary. The harmony which flows from their corporate life of grace prepares the home for change. The family is drawn deeper and deeper into the power and life of the Trinity. There is no end to this process. There is no perfection in this life—only when we reach our Father's house. Although we're always "on the way," God wants our journey to be happy and fruitful. He has provided everything we need to bring that about.

The unique gift which the Father provides for us is the grace to be priest, prophet, and kingly representative for our families. We are called to be *priest* for our home: one who offers sacrifice, labors to provide protection, and intercedes with God for our wife and children. As priest, we speak to God for our family and minister his blessings to those in our care. We provide material, spiritual, and emotional protection for them. We are called to be a *prophet*: one who speaks the word of God to others. A prophet gives testimony for God by his words and the witness of his life. He is a holy man. We also have a *kingly* role. As a son of royal blood, we are called to manage the affairs of our Father wisely. We are chief stewards of the spiritual and human resources placed in our care. As one under authority, we will be held accountable for our use of the king's gifts. "You, however, are a chosen race, a royal priesthood, a holy nation, a people he claims for his own to proclaim the glorious works of the one who called you from darkness into his marvelous light" (1 Pt 2:9).

We also share in Jesus' role of shepherd to his flock. He is the Chief Shepherd of the flock of man and the Lord of each household of the flock. But we are his assistants in this role, God's gift to our families. A father is not the Lord or the Shepherd, but rather a man who is commissioned by God to work with the Spirit in forming himself and others into images of the Almighty, reflections of his love.

The father in a Christian family also plays a critical role in God's wider plan of salvation. This plan envisions the renewal and restoration of all families and all mankind. A father's part in this overall effort begins as he takes his rightful place within the smallest unit of God's plan, the married couple. He and his wife form a pastoral team which is empowered to procreate and build the family. The family is conceived to be an earthly reflection of the unity and love which each person can look forward to in the eternal kingdom of God.

The family is a training ground, a school for shared life. The Christian home should be the place where we learn how to give of ourselves and love unconditionally. As this happens, the Christian family becomes a beacon for a dark world. It offers hope and a model for unity and peace. In fact, the family is the basic building block for the kingdom of God. It is our source of formation and strength. God's life springs forth from it. The Church has known this from the beginning and has always resisted anything which would undermine the Christian home, the basic cell of the Church.

The family is also a necessary unit in the Lord's call to evangelize the world. From healthy loving families will come the men and women who are equipped with hearts of service and a zeal for God's life. The witness of a shared life, centered on love, will draw others to Jesus and his good news. It is a vital expression of the Gospel in action.

The Christian father has a central role in this worldwide plan of evangelism. A changed father means a changed family. Changed families mean a changed, renewed Church. A renewed Church can speak with authority to a society in desperate need of truth and love. A rediscovery of the gift of Christian fatherhood will give hope to a world which is searching for truth. As the family goes, so goes the Church and the world.

Pope John XXIII made this point clearly in his encyclical, Ad Petri cathedram, a message to the couples and families of the world:

> For if peace, unity and harmony are not found in the home surroundings, how can they exist in civil society? Let the father of the family take the place of God among his children, and not only by his authority but by the upright example of his life also stand clearly in the first place. Within the walls of the home let there be an ardor of charity which existed among the family at Nazareth. Let all Christian virtues flourish, unity reign, examples of good life shine forth.

Why Isn't It Working?

After reading the preceding section, you may ask why families do not seem to work this way. The question comes naturally, since strong Christian families seem to be in such short supply in today's world.

There are many answers to this question. Every family is different, and the sources of their weakness are different. However, I believe there is a common basis to the problem. That basis is our damaged human nature and our tendency toward sin.

While grace calls and empowers us to live in the light, we still experience the effects of the darkness. We face a common enemy who has always sought to disrupt the love relationship between God and man. Satan, the master strategist, strikes the hardest at the enfleshment of that relationship, the family.

It is difficult for modern men to grasp and accept the spiritual realities of our fallen nature. We tend to take one of two extreme positions on the subject of sin and evil: We either take it too seriously and thereby become scrupulous and immobilized by fear, *or* we do not take it seriously enough, and dismiss Satan as an outmoded idea. Both extremes obscure God's truth. Here is what the scriptures say about these attitudes. Regarding fear: "Fear is useless. What is needed is trust" (Mk 5:36). Regarding neglect: "Keep careful watch over your conduct. Do not act like fools, but like thoughtful men. Make the most of the present opportunity, for these are evil days" (Eph 5:15-16). To these I would add a word from Pope Paul VI given during a general audience on November 15, 1973:

What are the greatest needs of the Church today? Do not let our answer surprise you as being over-simple or even superstitious and unreal: one of the greatest needs is defense from that evil which is called the Devil. That it is not a question of one devil but of many, is indicated by various passages in the Gospel (Lk 11:21; Mk 5:9). But the principal one is Satan, which means the Adversary, the Enemy; and with him many, all creatures of God, but fallen, because of their rebellion and damnation, a whole mysterious world, upset by an unhappy drama, of which we know very little.

The nature of sin—a failure to love—stems from our gift of free choice. The Father wants us to choose him freely. This means that we are also free *not* to choose him. We can direct our lives away from God, toward non-love and service of ourselves. All sin stems from pride, the manifestation of our basic rebellion against the Father, the dark side of our fallen nature. The most deceptive quality of sin is its ability to camouflage itself behind our giftedness. Man is infinitely resourceful in rationalizing his wrongdoing. Western man, being especially gifted with educational resources, is unusually adept at this. We tend to intellectualize our sin.

The truth is that sin is real and so is Satan, its originator. This once-glorious angel of Heaven wants to draw as many men as possible into his terrible fate of eternal separation from God.

Despite his lies, Satan has only as much power over us as we *choose* to give him. His power once allowed him to roam the world tempting, deceiving, and lying to whole nations. But at Calvary his reign came to an abrupt and permanent end:

> In Christ the fullness of deity resides in bodily form. Yours is a share of this fullness, in him who is the head of every principality and power. ...Even when you were dead in sin and your flesh was uncircumsised, God gave you new life in company with Christ. He pardoned all our sins. He canceled the bond that stood against us with all its claims, snatching it up and nailing it to the cross. Thus did God disarm the principalities and powers. He made a public show of them and, leading them off captive, triumphed in the person of Christ. (Col 2:9-10, 13-15)

If there is further doubt, let me say it clearly, Satan *is* defeated. He is only a fallen angel. He met his match in the person of Jesus.

While Satan is defeated, he still possesses great power, directed mainly through a body of followers which we call "evil spirits." They are that portion of the spirit world which followed him into rebellion against God and share his fate of exile and damnation. This body of satanic cohorts is hostile to the kingdom of God. They make every effort possible to draw men away from God into the kingdom which their leader promised them.

The spiritual realities of our fallen nature can be summed up simply: We are torn between two kingdoms. One has been defeated, is ultimately doomed, but is still fighting desperately for survival. The other kingdom has been established by Jesus and will last forever. Meanwhile, the two kingdoms are locked in combat. To realize the fullness of our inheritance, we will have to fight, much as our spiritual ancestors fought when they crossed the Jordan and took the promised land of Canaan. The Hebrews fought battles with flesh and blood foes. We engage evil in our minds and emotions.

To win this battle and realize God's promises, we must know

the nature of our enemy and be able to distinguish between friendly and foreign territory. The three signs of hostile forces are the "world," the "flesh," and the "devil" or "evil spirits."

"The world" is not natural creation, but instead refers to those man-made systems and environments which surround us. The values behind "the world" are individualism and independence from God. "The flesh" is not our bodies which God created and called good, but our fallen nature which draws us back into ourselves, into selfishness and lust. "Evil spirits" are Satan and his agents who deceive and tempt, always trying to turn us away from God's path. The world, the flesh, and the devil are the Christian father's adversaries. In Christ, a man fights against them to function effectively as the head of his family.

In our day, however, we have an additional problem: a technological society. Despite its benefits, our society—especially some of its economic and cultural features—is another major reason why it is so difficult to form a family based on God's truth.

For example, the media exalts a style of life and a set of values antagonistic to those described in the scriptures. The patterns of modern work remove a man from his home for many hours of the day. Mobility and economic pressures separate the nuclear family from the extended family of grandparents, relatives, and others who can support its life. Modern ideologies undermine the value of commitment and emphasize individualism and "self-fulfillment"—all to the detriment of a father who is trying to lead his family to unity and self-sacrificing love.

Our modern society can subtly suggest that family life is outmoded—a thing of the past. Some quotes from a national magazine will underline this kind of thinking. These are taken from an article forecasting expected change in the 1980s and its impact on our lives.

The number of individuals living alone, often as a result of divorce, is expected to increase more than any other category, up from less than 7 million in 1960 to more than 25 million by the end of the 1980s.

An appliance corporation executive predicts that most families will be short on time—not energy. He adds: "The family meal is a thing of the past. It's going the way of the family breakfast and the family lunch. To provide a variety of meals at various times during the day, households will buy more frozen and other processed foods that can be prepared quickly."

A professor of marketing and future environments believes the electronic home of the 1980s will be better suited to serve fast-moving families. Observing: "The home will become a filling station for people's needs, a place where parents and children can come and go and have their wants met, without having to depend so much on each other."

Jesus centered his teachings on the home, a meal, and time for each other. Now we are told they are obsolete. It's very clear that Christian families can expect little help or encouragement in the marketplace. Do we trust God or believe the "experts?"

This brief summary of "the problem" should not leave you fearful or discouraged, since God our Father has clearly stated that his promise is restoration, not condemnation. Being a good author, he has made his principal statement clearly, where we cannot miss it. In the first eleven chapters of Genesis, the opening book of the Bible, God's perspective of fallen humanity is clearly documented as: Creation, Election, Sin, and, ultimately, Restoration. Our Father will not abandon his children. His love is stronger than even death. His grace is assured to those who ask and receive.

The confident, well-equipped father who accepts both the promise and the problem is ready to move—on to the practical challenges of change. I can offer you hope. Success is achievable. The Lord can do it!

In the chapters that follow, I will attempt to share practical wisdom and spiritual insight. However, this book will not give you all the answers for your family. Only God can do that. Instead my hope is to lead you into asking yourself and God the right questions.

Here are six simple steps to follow while engaging the truth of the gospel and the practical experience which this book will offer:

1. Be honest.
2. Pray for faith.
3. Be still and listen to God. Don't move in confusion or guilt.
4. Ask for what you need. God will equip you.
5. Accept God's grace and trust it.
6. Do what you can. Expect God to do the rest.

CHAPTER TWO

Our Identity:
Son and Servant

St. Teresa of Avila taught us that, the first door to the Father's mansion is through self-knowledge. As I continue to follow Jesus, I find that statement is taking on more meaning. Before we can discover what God calls us to *do*, we must know who we *are* before him. The first door to the "Interior Castle" is awareness of our true identity.

Discovery of my true identity began several years ago when I was asked to give a talk on my relationship with God the Father. The outline I prepared stressed my desire for total dependence on the Father and the need to continually surrender the direction of my life to him. At that time, I had only begun this process, but the Holy Spirit was urging me to continue.

While writing that talk, I was asked to take a psychological test for corporate management in New York. The talk and the test pulled in opposite directions. I knew that the psychological profile of a successful executive needed to show traits such as corporate loyalty and aggressiveness, yet these were very different from the traits I was writing about in my talk. Was I going to tell the testing agency and my company what they wanted to hear, or be honest to a growing sense that my identity was unfolding as a son of God?

Anna helped me sort out the problem. She led me to the right question: "Who am I?" not "What do I want to do?" I struggled with that question for several weeks before my trip to New York. The answer finally came after a lunch break in the middle of the eight-hour battery of tests. The morning had been mostly on aptitude. The psychologist ended the session by saying, "Bob, go out and have a good lunch. Relax, because this afternoon we're going to ask some probing questions." While praying in my hotel room after lunch, the Lord cleared up my dilemma. He showed me who I am: a son of the Father, a husband, a father, and a worker in the world. That is my identity and the order of my priorities.

Returning for the remainder of those tests, I felt like a new man. The psychologist smiled and asked, "Who are you, Bob?" I told him, and the response shocked the good doctor. He knew that most men reaching for upward mobility had not asked themselves that question. It usually threw them off balance, exposing their insecurities. Years later, I had the opportunity to read the psychologist's report on my tests. The conclusion was "inconclusive." He had no box in which to categorize a spiritually renewed man, because my true identity flowed from God, not the corporation.

We gain our personal identity in Christ, through our relationship with Jesus—the crucified Lord. As an obedient son of the Father in heaven and Joseph, his human father, Jesus fulfilled the demands of his call, despite the cost. The seed of faith placed in our hearts at Baptism wants to flower so that we can identify with the life, death, and resurrection of Jesus. Our true identity can only be found in Christ. The following section describes the environment in which this happens.

The Kingdom of God

The Kingdom of God on earth was proclaimed with the enfleshing of God's word to man. It *has* come in Jesus and continues in Christ. Regardless of the ongoing tragedy of sin, the Kingdom is yet progressing. The reign of God on earth has translated a heavenly reality into human history. As we can sense the presence of God in our lives and in those around us, the Kingdom becomes real for us. Simply put, the Kingdom is God and his people in loving relationship.

The preaching of Jesus followed the words of John the Baptist.

Get ready! Prepare the way of the Lord! Jesus sent his disciples out with good news: The One the Israelites had waited and hoped for had come at last and was dwelling among them. Jesus' neighbors heard his words, but the revelation couldn't find root in their hearts because their image of the Kingdom didn't fit a carpenter from Nazareth. Their hopes were fixed on external political freedom and an earthly heritage. When Jesus revealed the Kingdom as an interior change in one's heart, most of the people rejected his message.

Do we do the same thing? What are your ideas and visions of the Kingdom of God? Let's look at the words of the Gospel. In the thirteenth chapter of Matthew, Jesus uses earthly analogies to explain a spiritual reality. The Kingdom of God is like a sower dropping seeds on various kinds of ground; weeds and good wheat growing together; a tiny mustard seed which flowers into a big shrub; a buried pearl for which a man would sell all he had; a net which was being let down to bring in all sorts of people and things. These are images of a slow but sure progression.

The Kingdom of God takes root in the soil of our hearts as we accept God's timetable for our lives, and resist despair over the human circumstances which clutter our spiritual harvest. As grace builds on the natural raw material we present to Jesus, so does the Kingdom become real when we accept the human condition in which it must progress. Those who want instant transformation and guarantees of security will miss the miracles of God being worked before their eyes. By human standards, the ways of God are not efficient, but they produce lasting results.

Living in the Kingdom is the call of every believer. It is life in Christ—our gift and our quest. Jesus insisted that the heavenly Father knows all our needs. "Set your hearts on his kingdom first, and on his righteousness, and all these other things will be given you as well" (Mt 6:33). We need to experience the Kingdom of God in our lives if we are to trust that God will do what he promises. The Lord has already planted a seed of faith in us. Our call is to nurture that seed.

Father Francis Martin has given a clear description of life in the Kingdom. He considers it "normal Christian living" and outlines it as:

1. Knowing Jesus personally.
2. Living in the conscious awareness of the power of the Holy Spirit.
3. Showing fruits of service, primarily evangelization and preaching of the word of God.
4. Living in community with others.
5. Having communities related in a perfect unity.

By those standards, very few of us are living in the fullness of the Kingdom. Rather, we are experiencing a progression toward an ideal. The Kingdom is *becoming*. The experience of living the Christian ideal is a hope which should grow in us; for now, our part is to do what we can to redirect our lives toward that ideal.

For most fathers, the Kingdom of God can become a living experience in at least two places: in our hearts and in our homes. Every father *can* personally commit himself to Jesus, and declare his home as part of the Kingdom. The quality of the soil in these two areas—heart and home—are definitely within our control. As we make decisions to build primary Christian relationships, we will experience the extended unity Fr. Martin describes as a norm and not an exception of the Christian life. We can begin by evangelizing ourselves and our households. Then, drawn into unity with other renewed families, we blend finally into a renewed Church, God's family of families.

Our Inheritance

The Kingdom of God has emerged over the centuries. Abraham received the seed of salvation for mankind when he was obedient and faithful to the Lord. Abraham was called to a new land and a new way of life. He was an immigrant in the land which God wanted to bless with a national identity. The fulfillment of that identity for us is the Kingdom of God on earth.

My grandparents were immigrants too. They were aliens,

coming to a strange land with hopes of peace and prosperity. They were willing to struggle with a new language, a new climate, ethnic intolerance, and other painful circumstances because they believed that this land was basically good and would someday offer full citizenship to their offspring. Similarly, the early generations of God's chosen people were aliens drawn on by the hope of good things to come. After almost 4000 years of wandering, struggling, and hoping, the promise reached its fulfillment in Jesus the Christ. He became the first citizen of God's Kingdom on earth. Through our brother, Jesus, we become co-heirs with him to the fullness of the Father's treasure, both here on earth and in glory to come.

Our inheritance is vast. It is passed on to us in both the *written* promises of God, as revealed to his people of past ages, and in the *living* word of the Church today. Our promise is one of full life, but it is delivered to us with a cover letter. The cover letter has only these words: "Pass it on!" We must live in the Kingdom of God with other people. Just as a seed must grow and eventually flower, so too the grace which comes to us must be passed on and bloom in others or it will become only dead principles.

There is no private salvation in the Kingdom. If there aren't "two or more," God is limited in dwelling among his people. As with the natural law of birth, life, and death, the Kingdom will eventually die on this earth when Jesus comes again. In that second Advent, Jesus will close the earthly prologue of the great salvation drama and open the one act which will last forever.

Our Identity Through the Cross

We will understand our identity as Christian fathers more clearly as we discover the meaning of the Cross in our lives. The work of the Cross contains the whole of God's saving action for his children, carried out in the life, death, and resurrection of Jesus Christ. Each of us must walk the same path as our master.

Although many fathers have experienced sacramental Baptism

and Confirmation, many need the ongoing conversion which is occuring through the renewal movements of the Church. Our walk in faith is usually quickened by an adult "yes" to God. This release of God's love corresponds to the early ministry of Jesus: The blind were given sight, the lame walked, prisoners were released from their cells. Emotions are high and nothing seems to be able to diminish our hunger for God.

Our season of miracles buries the seed of faith more deeply into the rich soil of our hearts. The emotions of a personal experience of God can last for some time, but they are not a base upon which a Christian father can sustain his call or discover his identity before God. Like the Master, we must push on into desert places and eventually into a confrontation with sin and disorder.

For Jesus, the road led from Nazareth to Bethany to Jerusalem to Calvary. Facing Calvary meant a realization of pain, death, and unknowing. We face the same facts as we allow the Lord to reveal his plan for us. As Jesus knelt at Gethsemane, he asked if there was another way, only to receive the assurance and strength to keep going. Our walk with the Lord deepens with every decision to submit our lives to the Father's will, not our own, making the Word of God our standard and our guarantee. At various points in our relationship with God, we stop trying to sell him on our plan and fully accept his.

That kind of surrender doesn't happen quickly. The Apostles struggled to turn the Lord back to the time of miracles, but Jesus admonished them. When Peter, the one he had chosen to lead, tried to stop the Lord, Jesus said, "Get out of my sight, you satan!" (Mt 16:23). He didn't mince words with his followers, but told them exactly what to expect. He kept his face pointed to Jerusalem. He knew his mission. So must we.

Following his final surrender at Calvary, Jesus' body lay quietly in a tomb for a few days. However, while the body of the crucified Lord was still and lifeless, his spiritual victory over the forces of hell and the vindication of past believers was being accomplished. It was during this apparently dormant period that the real power of the Cross was released.

For the Christian father who has experienced full initiation into a life in the Spirit and has faced himself and his sin, the time of patient waiting for God to accomplish his plan is crucial. For me, the dormant period meant stepping back from spiritual "activities" to discover what God was saying. It was a desert time of quiet listening, a time to face the changes that were needed in my daily life. I liked the miracles and the glory of serving the Lord externally; the call to repentance, transformation, and inner healing made me uneasy. A good friend and spiritual counselor, Father Dan Cavanaugh, put it very clearly to me. He said, "Bob, most people don't grow into Christian maturity because they refuse to face Calvary where they live." The cross was not "out there;" it was in my heart and in my home.

A deeper commitment to the Lord follows each surrender of our will. The man who allows God to plan his life will emerge from the quiet time of listening, deeper in faith, and ready to serve with joy. As we allow God to complete his work in us, we become "new creations," men who are useful to God in furthering the Kingdom on earth. Our old ways of thinking and acting are changed. Conversion to Jesus has penetrated to the marrow of our personhood, our motives, and our attitudes—the inner forces which tell us who we are and how we should behave. To become useful for God—in a family or in a wider arena—this kind of change must happen.

Our identity emerges in times of change and periods of rest. The knowledge of who we are frees us to embrace our call from the Father. As we walk through deeper cycles of conversion, we become increasingly aware of our true identity as sons of God and servants of the King.

These two facets of our identity—sonship and servanthood—become the timber of our personal cross. They lead us into resurrection and glory. The next two sections will deal with sonship and servanthood—the vertical and the horizontal dimensions of that cross.

Sonship

The first aspect of our identity is sonship—the vertical dimension of the Cross of Jesus. Through the saving power of the cross, we enjoy an intimate relationship with our creator. Jesus taught us not to say "the" Father but "our" Father—"Abba." This word can be translated as "Daddy!" In our relationship with God's only son, we also become acceptable as sons.

Since Jesus used the term "father" to describe our God, we can gain some insight into the mind of God by reflecting on human fatherhood. Through our understanding and experience of fatherhood, we can begin to realize what the heavenly Father looks to and hopes for in a son.

When I became a natural father, I changed. A part of the old, selfish man in me died and was replaced by something of God's nature. It was more than paternity. Ralph Martin, a leader in Church renewal, has said that "father graces" began to flow into him when he saw his first child. I know what he means. When I became a father, my heart leaped and rejoiced with new vigor as those "father graces" flowed.

The awakening of fatherhood led me to begin asking new questions. I asked myself: "How much do I love these children of mine?" "What do I want for them?" "How should they relate to me?" My answers to these questions gave me some sense of God the Father's love and desires for us, his children. Pondering these questions, I could see how God wanted me, as a son, to be hungry for knowledge of him; obedient to his word; trusting in his care; willing to pass on the life he has shared with me. Let's consider these qualities of sonship in more detail.

Hunger

The first sign of the Spirit's stirring in a son's heart is a hunger for knowledge of God. During a very difficult time in my life, after my father's death, my son Rob asked, "Dad, does God wear a belt?" Rob was crushed at the death of his grandfather, and he wanted to know more about this God who took him away. Did he use a belt to punish us? I was unable to answer Rob's question. Realizing I was empty in my spirit, the questioning eventually led me closer to the Lord. God places a hunger for him in his sons, and he also promises to satisfy this hunger. Jesus said, "Would one of you hand his son a stone when he asks for a loaf, or a poisonous snake when he asks for a fish? If you, with all your sins, know how to give your children what is good, how much more will your heavenly Father give good things to anyone who asks him!" (Mt 7:9-11).

Obedience

I want my children to be attentive and obedient to me. My son's ability to listen to my voice and obey will bring blessings to him. Obedience is a trait which the military taught me well. In a combat situation, a man must respond obediently in order to stay alive. The spiritual combat which a son of God faces every day is more subtle, but no less deadly than the wars of man.

To develop the gift of submission and obedience in my children, I pay special attention to shaping their attitudes, not just their external behavior. Since I want willing obedience in my own children, I know my Father also wants me to develop a supple inner sense which bends easily to his perfect will.

Trust

I want my children to believe what I say to them. They must develop a *radical* trust in their father's word. I have tried to earn their trust by fulfilling my promises whenever that is possible. Our heavenly Father has never broken his promise; as his sons we can place complete trust in the word he speaks to us. The Cross was essential in communicating that word to us, since it proves in flesh and blood how far God's love for man will go.

A son's trust in his father must bring him beyond what his eyes can see into what his heart demands. A child will demonstrate this virtue by leaping without fear from a staircase into his father's waiting arms. There is no doubt in the child's mind that his father will bring him to safety. We can build the same trust that our Father will catch us when he calls for a leap of faith.

Passing on Life

When a father has poured human and spiritual life into his children, he wants to see that life passed on to posterity. We want to pass on our inheritance. It's a joy for a man to see his grandchildren and be assured that the wisdom, blessing, and experiences which have made up his life will be carried on into time. I've watched this interaction between our children and their grandfather.

Our Father in Heaven also wants his earthly sons to pass on his life to our children. Our Father wants to pour faith, hope, and love into us, to equip us as fathers who can pass his life on to others. His desire is to see our children build their personal relationship with him, since God has only children, not grandchildren.

One scene from the recent TV series "Roots" captured this desire of the Father. The hero's grandfather showed him a cross-section of a giant tree. He explained how each individual life span was only a speck in the mind of God; how the life of the family was the lasting reality. We have desires like this for our children. The Father has the same kind of desire for us.

These are the essential attributes of sonship which have come to me as I've looked at my own children and my love for them. I'm sure you could add some of your own—think about it. In searching out the desires of your human fatherhood, you will touch on God's mind and his hopes for your sonship.

Servanthood

Indelibly printed on our summons to fatherhood is also a call to service. When a person commits himself to a vocation—whether it is marriage, priesthood, or living single for the Lord—the grace of service is stirred and increased. Our conversion progresses as we make a mature commitment to care

for other people and realize that service in love is a joy, not a
burden.

The call to serve the Lord resounds through the Old and
New Testaments. The Jewish people exhorted the priests, servants of the temple, during their night watch, "Come, bless
Yahweh, all you who serve Yahweh" (Ps 134:1). Service, whatever our state, is part of every man's call. It is the horizontal
bar of our Christian cross.

In a modern society, it is easy to miss the scriptural meaning
of service and the dignity attached to it. As men of God, we are
offered the privilege to serve with the Lord and care in a special way for God's children. However, in today's society, the
joy of personally serving another is replaced in many cases by
machines and appliances. If we strive to climb the ladder of
success, we expect to be served, not to serve. Today we can
purchase things or hire people to do almost anything for us.
No wonder we have trouble understanding Jesus' identity as
the suffering servant prophesied by Isaiah. He instructs us to
follow him in dropping our desires for power and control.
"You know how those who exercise authority among the
Gentiles lord it over them; their great ones make their importance felt. It cannot be like that with you. Anyone among you
who aspires to greatness must serve the rest, and whoever
wants to rank first among you must serve the needs of all"
(Mt 20:25-27). Our call to fatherhood could not have been put
more directly. We are not the lords of our castles, but servants
of our families, co-workers with Jesus.

Imitating Jesus

Jesus is a master who serves with his followers. He teaches
us to reach out to others and let go of ourselves. We can expect
him to meet all our needs as we busy ourselves in loving service. Jesus displayed this commitment to us in the clearest way
possible in the upper room, when he took on the towel and
bowl of the Jewish house servant and washed the dirty feet of
his disciples.

A good friend once told me that I was a very fortunate man.

He said, "To be married and to serve the Lord is the greatest joy on earth." That is something every Christian father can experience when he sees his vocation as service to God, not just to man. It is our privilege to serve the Lord.

Serving our families for Jesus means serving *in his name*. That involves going about our daily tasks the way he would, with his mind and heart. The best word I've heard for this is "tending." We should serve our families in the same way Jesus tended his flock.

Above all, serving in the name of Jesus is more than just accomplishing good things for God. So often we bring the corporate agenda home, looking upon our service as completing holy jobs rather than caring and loving the people with whom we interact. Jesus is concerned about the total person—body, mind, and spirit. God is calling for fellow servants with Jesus, empowered by the Holy Spirit to challenge the ways of man with the Good News that is Christ.

In his name we can chant with the psalmist, "I bind myself to do your will; Lord do not disappoint me. I will run the way of your commands; you give freedom to my heart" (Ps 119:30-32).

Serving the Larger Family

Jesus' earthly ministry was confined to a few miles of territory in the Middle East, and he spent a good deal of time personally training his apostles to carry on his work. After his ascension, the Father sent the Spirit to enable his followers to bring the good news to the world. As servants of the gospel, this is also our call. Although our primary service is to lead one family, God wants our witness of love and unity to be carried into the body of his church. This will come through the witness of spiritually renewed families, a fruit which will stem from Christian fathers who understand their gifts and their call. The Church needs this charism of spiritual leadership in a family. The ordained priesthood cannot effectively pastor God's people without the full cooperation, support, and active participation of a renewed laity and regenerated families.

To be a servant to the church of Christ, we must acquire knowledge. The gift of the Spirit is for our edification, not just for enthusiasm. A base of solid spiritual teaching will allow us to be useful to the shepherds of the church and to serve more effectively.

With knowledge comes responsibility for the real Church, not just those elements which make us comfortable. A servant must be ready to move into the part of his master's household which has the greatest need at the time. The new pastoral plan for family ministry in the Church, published by the U.S. Catholic Conference, is an excellent tool for the groundwork of lay ministry by married couples, single parents, and children. Most of the ministry for families called for in that plan is intended to come from other families. We are being directed to reach out to those in the Church around us. A servant of God is stirred by need and acts on his own initiative.

Although Jesus caused turmoil in the religious circles of his land, he was obedient and respectful of the civil authority of the Roman government. He could have marshalled the forces of heaven to destroy Rome in an instant, yet he chose to set an example of respect for civil government. As a servant in his Kingdom, we must follow his lead. We should not be indifferent to the secular world which surrounds us or to the rightfully appointed civil government which serves the human needs of all God's people. Peter wrote to the Church, "Because of the Lord, be obedient to every human institution, whether to the emperor as sovereign or to the governors he commissions for the punishment of criminals and the recognition of the upright" (1 Pt 2:13-14). We cannot witness to a faithless world if we are not faithful to the little things of good citizenship, honest employment, and community service. We must fight the tendency of some spiritual men to become lax in our civil duties and uncooperative with non-believers.

Part of the early Church fell into this error. Some people said, "Why bother with the material concerns of life." Parousia-fever is often the escape of the lazy man, who can avoid work with the excuse that the Lord is coming soon. Jesus wants us to work and enjoy the blessings of life. When he returns, he wants to find us with our sleeves rolled up, not hiding under the covers. The servant of God is a man of civil and spiritual responsibility. .

At the same time, a servant of the Lord can expect some rejection and persecution because, by definition, he is not "of this world." Although his hands move to serve today's need, his heart is motivated by an eternal reality, which dominates petty cares. He can laugh and enjoy life despite its troubles and concerns.

Although he works with a hope for reasonable human success and some comfort for his family, the man of God is not tied to the struggle for upward mobility which drains his neighbors. He is a servant who is happy with his lot. This visible inner peace is often resented by those set on power and status. Try as he may to love his unbelieving neighbors, he will probably be called "a religious fanatic." The Christian father is a worldly contradiction. He will do menial things with a smile, praising God for allowing him the right to serve his family, his Church, and the world which God created.

Now that we've drawn a clearer picture of the identity of a Christian father, you may be thinking—"That's awfully abstract! How do I put my identity as a son of God and a servant of the Kingdom into action?" The next section will provide you with some answers.

Part II

Priorities

CHAPTER THREE

Fruitful Interaction: Priorities, Relationships, and Decisions

My good friend, Fr. Dom Rossi, has a favorite parable he uses to explain heaven and hell. He says that heaven and hell look quite similar. In each place banquets are set with fine food and drink, so delicious and plentiful that it staggers the imagination. However, in both places those at the table must eat with five-foot-long spoons!

In hell, the five-foot spoons cause continual frustration; try as they might, no one can quite fit them into their mouths. They greedily stuff the spoons to overflowing with goodies, but they can't eat the food. By contrast, the five-foot spoons present no problem in heaven; there, no one feeds himself. Each person has already learned to expect God to care for him, so he busies himself feeding others. The King's servants constantly refill the banquet table and everyone is well cared for.

The point of the parable is this: Those who are bound for the heavenly banquet have learned to forget themselves and to reach out to the needs of others. As we learn this principle, we are fitting into God's plan for his Kingdom. Each facet of creation is brought into fullness through its interaction with someone or something else. We, like the natural creation, are willed by God to be *dependent*. God has created man to need him and others in order to be complete. When we ignore this principle and try to be self-sufficient, our troubles begin.

Priorities in the Kingdom of God are relationships—not things or tasks. God wants our relationships as fathers of our families to demonstrate the unity of heaven on earth. To possess the full fruits of the Kingdom, we must know God's order of priority for our relationships and make the decisions necessary to support that order.

God's Priorities

Our first priority is to seek the Kingdom of God. This becomes a lived reality as we experience fruitful Christian relationships. Our experience of the Kingdom grows from seeds of faith, hope, and love which the Spirit plants in us. These seeds are usually carried to us by those believers around us. These tiny seeds are meant to grow into the visible fruit of a changed life—a life which has God at its center. The pain and frustration many Christians feel come when the potential in our seeds of faith, hope, and love is never realized.

A Christian father's greatest desire is to reproduce the human and spiritual goodness in himself. As he sees that happening, he feels his basic drives are being fulfilled. When the opposite occurs—when the weaknesses in his own life are transferred to his family—a father is often plagued with self-hatred and guilt. A source of the emotional withdrawal and spiritual failure that afflict many men is this feeling of frustrated fatherhood.

A man's greatest joy is to see himself being carried into posterity. When this happens, his role as co-creator with God is affirmed and satisfied. Meaningful relationships produce peace and harmony within us. These are established as we take what God has given us, allow it to grow to maturity, then pass it on to others. We fathers will not be able to interact fruitfully with our families or others if we are not at peace within ourselves and with God.

When sin or disorder is being nurtured in us, our fruit of changed life becomes stunted, like a beautiful citrus crop which is exposed to a sudden frost. The seed is frozen and never realizes its potential. Fruitlessness becomes our greatest pain.

Sometimes our lives seem like the formless wasteland or darkened abyss described in the first verses of Genesis. This happens when we withdraw into a cave of "self" away from the "wind" of the Spirit which brings order to creation (Gn 1:2). God has not withdrawn from us; we have withdrawn from him. The solution is to turn around and head back toward God's light and his cleansing Spirit. Scripture calls this turning back to God "repentance." To return to a fruitful life, where our priorities and relationships are directed by the Spirit, we need only to decide to change; God will do the rest.

Union and Unity

The first tangible change which God wants for fathers is to develop a personal communion with him. Union with God is the beginning and the end of our identity as the Father's children. When the Jews wanted to know what was most important for them, Jesus restated Moses' words: "Hear O Israel! The Lord our God is Lord alone! Therefore you shall love the Lord your God with all your heart, with all your soul, with all your mind, and with all your strength" (Mk 12:29-30). The first priority for the believer is to love God with his total person. This is how we (the branches) make contact with Jesus (the vine). The life of the Father is brought to us through the intercession of Jesus and the power of the Holy Spirit.

This relationship can take many external forms, but regardless of style, we call it "prayer." It means speaking, then listening to God and receiving his word for us. We will deal with prayer in some detail in a later chapter, but here I want to emphasize its importance as the first priority for fathers. A father is first of all a child of God. He must sit before the Father to be taught and loved.

Many men busy themselves doing good things for God in an attempt to love him. However, in prayer, we discover that God's love is not earned; it is simply received. We love God by accepting his Son Jesus and the gift of the Spirit he offers. Loving God does not mean doing holy things, but receiving the One who *is* holy. "Love, then, consists of this: not that we have loved God, but that he has loved us and has sent his Son as an offering for our sins" (1 Jn 4:10).

Union with God is the first part of the Great Commandment. The second part, Jesus said, is like it. "You shall love your neighbor as yourself." John also presented this part of his master's teaching in his first epistle: "Beloved, if God has loved us so, we must do the same for one another. No one has ever seen God. Yet if we love one another God dwells in us, and his love is brought to perfection in us" (1 Jn 4:11-12). Unity with our neighbor is the practical call of a follower of Jesus.

You might ask, "What does *unity* mean in human relationships?" Jesus' words "as yourself" tell us that our first unity must be with ourselves. We must be spiritually, physically, emotionally, and intellectually at peace in order to love others. Fruitful relationships begin by doing whatever is necessary to love our most difficult neighbor—ourselves.

We have to accept our personhood as made and loved by God. We are formed in his image and likeness, despite the coating of pain, hurt, and fear which covers his creation. Jesus goes past that covering, seeing us as we really are. He would say, "You're my brother. Come back home with me and I will teach you to love even yourself." We must accept ourselves despite our past failure, expecting that Jesus can build on the basic goodness which lies within.

The order of priorities now begins to take shape:

—Union with God is always the first.
—Unity with my neighbor is next.
—A healthy love of my true personhood is intermingled in both.

If these are the primary relationships for a Christian father, why are they so difficult? Why is it so hard to persevere in prayer? Why do we often fail to love ourselves? Why do we struggle to relate intimately with those closest to us? I believe the main reason is our need for total honesty in these relationships, and our unwillingness to go beyond a safe, superficial level.

The fear that we won't be accepted and loved for ourselves is really part of our damaged human condition; it is not God's plan. He wills that we live in union with him and with other people despite our sinfulness and fear of rejection. His plan contains provision for overcoming and healing our inability to relate in love. In fact, there is a sense in which healing of our relationships *is* God's plan. His work is always to unite what man has divided.

Our part is to pray for God's healing and to honestly deal with that which obstructs our relationships. We can rely on Jesus' promises. He calls us to personal holiness (perfection in grace) and to complete unity among men: "That all may be one" (Jn 17:21). Jesus offers us a promise and a challenge. Only in him will we find the power to change those patterns in us which close us off from the Father and our brothers and sisters. Jesus lifts our eyes from the inadequacy of our fallen humanity and says that better ways are possible, if we place our trust in him and do what he tells us to.

Who Is My Neighbor?

Fathers have great responsibilities to many other people. It is natural to ask "Who is my neighbor?" For answers, I want you now to take the time to read carefully two parables which Jesus used to teach us about our neighbors: The Good Samaritan (Lk 10:25-37) and The Last Judgment (Mt 25:31-46). Some simple answers begin to emerge from both readings.

In each story, there is someone in genuine *need*. The man Luke describes as beaten and half dead, and those Matthew describes as naked, hungry, in prison, and lonely, needed someone else to help them.

Second, in both parables, someone is able to help. There is *proximity* between the need and the believer. The priest and the Levite walked past the man lying half dead on the road from Jerusalem to Jericho. The Samaritan responded. The personal call to feed, clothe, and free your neighbor is only possible if you can touch that person. Although support for foreign missions, clothing drives, and intercessory prayer also respond to the scriptures, our primary call involves face-to-face encounters.

The third similarity in the parables is the call to *do what we can*. God does not ask us to give more than we have, nor to think we have less than we really do. Rather, if we are following God, we are assured that "my grace is sufficient" (2 Cor 12:9), and "He will not let you be tested beyond your strength" (1 Cor 10:13). The good Samaritan didn't completely meet the wounded man's need; he did what he could. Those in Matthew 25 who will enter the Kingdom are the ones who did something and were amazed at Jesus' delight with the little they did. Only God can meet all our needs. We are called to do what we can.

For Christian fathers, the closest people who we can touch, and who have a need which we can meet, are those in our natural families: wife, children, and parents. They are our first neighbors. The unity which God wants should occur in these primary relationships first. They are the fertile soil in which our seeds of faith can take root and flower into visible, lasting fruit. This fruit can also affect a wider arena.

As the Christian family goes, so goes the church and society. The renewal of the family begins when we learn to see all people through God's eyes, especially those under our roof who are starving spiritually and emotionally, if not materially. As our primary relationships move into God's order, the Lord will open and prepare the apostolic soil of community and Church for the seeds coming from a family living their faith. This provides us with something precious to offer. When there is peace at home, a father is able to ask, "What can I bring to my Church?"

Although the soil of the natural family is fertile, we cannot till it alone. God knows our labor is difficult, but it is exactly the way he intended it. He created the family so there could be no lasting relationship outside of him. God must be a part of any human family if it is to live in peace and exercise its call to witness to a world in bondage to individualism and materialism. In fact, this life of selfless love and unity in relationship is the apostolic mission of the Christian family.

Renewing Your Sphere of Influence

The ever-widening circles of relationship which God intends us to touch with his love can be described as our "sphere of influence." We can visualize that sphere as a globe of the world which our children have in most of their classrooms. Children like to find a point on that globe and say, "Here's where we are." Try imagining a sphere constructed of people instead of sheet metal. You are one point on the surface; surrounding you are your natural family and parents. These primary relationships make up the first ring around you on your sphere of influence. Other rings flow out from your center, making up a large body of people which your life will touch and affect in some way.

Consider how your "sphere of influence" changes over time. When you are born, the globe is very small. Your world is contained within very few relationships. As a baby, the center of your world is really yourself; the "others" who surround you emphasize that self-centeredness. Your sphere is filled with "self." This condition is our original self-centeredness. If you think infants are innocent, observe twins in a crib together fighting over the same toy or a bottle. Yes, we are born with our natures distorted and with a real capacity for selfishness and sin.

Critical changes occur in this sphere of influence when we present that child to God at Baptism. The seed of God's life is planted in his heart and the *potential* for change is opened. Now the process of conversion to Jesus begins in a tangible way. The center of the child's sphere has shifted from self to God. The Holy Spirit gives us the power to begin driving out selfishness and he infills the void within us. The Spirit stirs us, creating a hunger which can only be satisfied by his indwelling. Although a tendency toward sin still occupies our sphere, the medium within it has begun to change. Through that medium, we begin to touch others on the surface of our sphere. Before conversion began we did this mostly to "get something" for ourselves. We were still self-centered. As conversion progresses, our original condition is radically changed.

Paul described the change in our global center from self to God as "the groaning of creation" (Rom 8:22). The groaning is not just a semantic leap in Paul's language; it is an accurate description of the pain which conversion brings to our old life of sin and pride. Conversion is a process. Changing the center of our lives is painfully slow.

When we make an adult "yes" to God, the balance of power in the center of our sphere shifts noticeably. We're now free to interact with others more *through God* than through self since he is filling our void. This is more than a theological concept; our personality and our interior drives actually become tied to our spiritual center. As we begin relating to others through God, people can sense a difference in how we interact with them. They can "see" Jesus in us. Our actions now say, "How may I love you?" not, "What can you do for me?"

This ongoing process of death to self leads to the ultimate conversion—sainthood. That tiny mustard seed of faith, carried by the power of the Spirit into our heart, is fired with a drive toward sanctity. Our part is a daily decision to cooperate with conversion. How well we learn to be obedient to the promptings of the Holy Spirit determines how deep and how far our change can progress.

If only our exterior habits change, that conversion is only a partial "renewal." This means we've changed the most obvious patterns of sin; we've whitewashed the outside of the sphere. Jesus spoke to this kind of conversion when he told the Pharisees and Scribes: "First cleanse the inside of the cup so that its outside may be clean" (Mt 23:26). At the center of our sphere are the motives and attitudes which make up our interior drives.

As conversion works its way deeply into our person and the center of our sphere is converted by God's Word, restoration of a soul begins. This is the cleansing which God wants inside a man—a total purging of the old self, externally and deep within. As this happens we become truly useful to God. We can reflect Jesus and his caring love for others. We can give genuine healing and life-giving hope. Our priorities, the people God has placed on our sphere, can now be served by a son who is focused on their well-being, whose service is directed by the Spirit.

Decisions—The Practical Effects

Questions remain: How do fathers establish the relationships God wants for them? What practical decisions should we make?

For instance: How should I spend my money? What thoughts should occupy my mind? How should I manage my time? Our answers to questions like these reveal our true priorities and show us how they affect our lives.

Simply put, our priorities are what influence our practical decisions. Even though we don't realize it, the mind decides and acts according to the true priorities which we live with. Despite our sincere intentions, it's what we *decide and then do* that really counts.

The decision process must begin with an assignment of clear priorities to the relationships on our sphere of influence. I have found an excellent discussion of this in *Maximum Marriage* by Tim Timmons. Timmons exhorts us to "cultivate" the following areas, and he cites our priorities in this order:

Priority 1 - A personal relationship with the Lord.

Priority 2 - A personal relationship with your spouse.

Priority 3 - Personal relationships with your children.

Priority 4 - Personal relationships inside the body of Christ.

Priority 5 - Personal relationships outside the body of Christ.

Priority 6 - Personal ministry relationships.

You might ask where your job fits in this scale of relationships. This depends on whether you work in an environment of Christian believers. Most fathers must spend significant amounts of time in a non-Christian work environment, but chiefly in order to provide support for priorities 2 and 3. This is not wrong; however, fathers need not go beyond the bounds of normal employment to build relationships on the job.

Many practical consequences flow from these priorities. Our most important relationships are those that are closest to us on our sphere of influence. The priority diminishes as distance increases. Now we can establish a rule for the decision-making process: *Our decisions must always support our highest priorities.* The decisions you make about job, ministry, hobbies, entertainment, etc., should positively influence the most important people in your life.

In other words, a Christian father is not free to make decisions and commitments only according to their effect on himself. If he is going to interact in love with God, family, neighbors, Church, and others, he must seriously consider the impact of his decisions on those relationships.

At the same time, God will never deny us the material means we need to be a good husband and father. He wants us to have employment which will bring out our natural gifts and also provide adequately for our family. However, we should view our work as just that, not as our top priority. When a work situation begins to encroach on our highest priorities— God and family—it's time for a closer look at the job. We should have the same attitude toward other interests, such as sports, personal hobbies, and even our service to Church or community. We should be constantly asking the question: "How will this affect the people closest to me and my relationship with God?"

Fathers will often have to make difficult decisions and re-evaluate past commitments. At such times, go first to God for wisdom. Take a clear objective look at the positive and negative effects of each decision, and determine what the Lord thinks about it.

Let me illustrate this point by relating a personal experience. A few years ago I was a rapidly rising young salesman in my company, located in Philadelphia, working hard to develop that territory. I was ambitious. However, when I came into a personal relationship with Jesus about eight years after starting this job, it became clear that my priorities needed a good bit of adjustment.

Although much of my personal energy and attention had been focused on climbing the corporate ladder of success, I had excused this strain and sacrifice, as many men do, by repeating over and over, "I'm only doing it for my family." Strangely enough, as my goals were reached, I didn't find peace or contentment; only new, higher, and more demanding goals. I had bought the great American dream and found it a constant struggle. My family suffered. Although I was now able to provide more material goods for Anna and the kids, the husband and father they needed was not around very much.

As the center of my life slowly shifted to God, the folly of my direction surfaced. I was out of God's order, yet I did not know what to do. One day, in my confusion, I prayed, "Jesus, I don't understand what's wrong, but will you help me straighten it out?" I didn't comprehend how well God hears an honest prayer. Soon something happened that forced the issue into the open.

My priority in life all along had been to reach a top executive position in our company. Now I was offered a lucrative job as manager of our New York office, leading eventually to election as an officer of the corporation. The dream had come true. I accepted immediately, without much thought and with no prayer.

My wife and children had a different reaction. When I explained our great opportunity to them, they showed none of the excitement I expected. They asked silly questions like, "Where will we live?" and "Will we ever see you?" They had obviously missed the point: A man couldn't turn down an opportunity like this. The tension between Anna and I rose to a breaking point, until she finally consented to go. Her surrender left me only one hurdle to cross: The growing conviction in my heart that I was making a serious mistake.

One day I buried my head in my hands and cried out, "Lord, help me!" Suddenly I remembered my earlier prayer to Jesus for help in straightening out my life. God let me know unquestionably that he had brought me to this place to define what was important. From that moment, it was clear I had to reverse my decision, but I was afraid. What would happen to me? What a fool I'd appear to be. Again I prayed, "Lord, are you a part of this?" Feeling his peace and assurance, I picked up the telephone immediately, called the president of my company, and told him simply that I had made a mistake and couldn't accept the company's offer. This call was hard to make. I was prepared to be fired on the spot. Instead, he paused momentarily and then said kindly, "Bob, I don't understand your reasons, but I know you're sincere. Don't worry; we'll work it out."

That was a pivotal point in my life. Had I carried out my human decision and not yielded to the Spirit, I'm sure my life would be far different today. As it was, God blessed my obedience with material and spiritual abundance. I also established a level of honesty with my employer which allowed me to share my new life in Christ with him.

That decision taught me how to approach important changes in my life. Now I know enough to ask these questions:

1. Will this change bring me closer to Jesus?
2. How will the change affect Anna and the kids?
3. How will it give me support in my Christian life?
4. How will it affect local believers?

These questions are relevant to all important decisions—from moving to take a new job, to invitations to serve the Lord in ministry. No matter how holy or attractive it may seem, a father must ask what effect new commitments will have on his primary relationships. Remember, God wants abundant life in Christ for us. He will not lead us into frustration and confusion. If you find yourself confused, look at some of your past decisions and ask the question: Does this decision support my highest priorities?

Unity in relationships isn't easy. Neither is union with God. Both require decisions for life and death to self. If these decisions seem to be the most difficult to make in our intimate relationships, that's exactly how God has planned it. He doesn't want us to become independent, but obedient to him. To grow in union with God and unity with our neighbor, we must follow his plan of loving interaction. We are to be first in relationship with God, and then go "through him" into oneness with the others in our lives.

A Christian father must have clearly defined priorities. These priorities are the people in his life, viewed through God's perspective. When he is faced with decisions, his first thought must be "Who?" not "What?" will be affected. God and people are the priorities in the Kingdom.

CHAPTER FOUR

How To Begin:
Shifting Priorities

My friend Bud managed a successful Little League baseball team. He generously gave considerable time and energy to help his son and other boys learn to play baseball well. Bud and I worked together. Although he was a fine salesman, I couldn't imagine how he could have the patience to put up with the frustrations that went with coaching. One day I asked him, "Bud, how do you do it? How do you teach those kids to play baseball?" Bud's answer was short and to the point. He said, "It's easy, I just stick to basics. Smart base running. Sliding, bunting. Don't swing at bad pitches. Get the ball over the plate. We drill these things for hours." I asked him if that got boring. "Sure," he said, "but that's the only way to learn. The kids try fancy tricks, but they learn that my way works best. We won a state championship because we knew the fundamentals."

I've often thought about Bud's advice. He didn't bother with fancy techniques or programs, but concentrated on the fundamentals. Many professional coaches do the same thing. When their team is in a slump or when their star is not hitting, what do they do? The same thing Bud did—back to basics! They don't try elaborate new schemes. Instead, they concentrate on doing the basic things well.

This practical wisdom can be helpful to a father. He's on God's team, and at times he gets into a slump too. The harder he tries to manage himself and his family, the worse things seem to get. When a man's life feels out of balance and his family seems like a burden, he needs a new approach. His coach is God and the advice he'd receive would probably sound like this: "Son, I love you, and I see how hard you're trying; but for now, you have to concentrate on the fundamentals for a while."

A father can expect to receive the best possible coaching. When his priorities are out of order, he can look to God to bring him back to what is essential. The most important part of this process is its beginning. A Christian father begins to refocus his life by first discovering his actual priorities and then asking God to help him put them into the right order.

Back to Basics

The basic elements of our Christian life are prayer, study, and loving action. These are also the three fundamentals that have to be present for a man to experience the fullness of his call as a Christian father. The Cursillo, a movement for renewal, teaches that these three elements can be thought of as the legs of a tripod. The tripod is a strong structure, but only if it is built in a certain way. The legs of the Christian father's tripod are prayer, study, and loving action. Each makes up one part of the support system we need. To remain stable, the legs have to be strong, steady, and of the right length. If one is shaky or out of symmetry with the others, a man's life tends to become unbalanced.

For this tripod to support our life, it has to stand on solid ground. If its foundation is weak or uncertain, our lives will begin to collapse. The tripod of prayer, study, and action must sit squarely on the written and the living word of God. This means our lives must be based solidly on scripture and the teaching of the Church. The tripod model is a good one, but many—perhaps most—fathers still find themselves in an unbalanced condition. Something is weak. Their lives feel shaky. The foundation is uncertain. In this case, which leg of the tripod should we repair first? What sequence do we use in trying to establish the basics of fatherhood?

A good principle to follow is that loving actions should follow prayer and study. A father's life starts to come into order when his thoughts, plans, and behavior flow out of a regular prayer life and a good study program. The three basic elements of fatherhood all work together, but prayer and study must come first if our actions are to be inspired by God and in line with his plan for us.

This three-pronged support gives us a new and a secure perspective on the life around us. We're sitting on a stool which isn't shaking. As our basic security is established, we can concentrate on how we relate to the others whom God has put into our lives. Our principal underpinning is the confidence that we are loved by the Father and that we are sons in the family of God; now we must shift our attention off ourselves and onto our relationships. Our action, although loving, must line up with a correct set of relationship priorities. We may be doing the right things, but are our actions reflecting God to the people closest to us? Is the motivating force behind our interaction the Holy Spirit and Christian principles, or has humanism taken hold of us?

These are crucial questions. A return to the basics—prayer, study, and loving action—also involves a shift in our attention from the world to God. Do we know God? Do we reflect him to those around us? If we can be compared to a mirror on the tripod of prayer, study, and action, in what direction are we pointing and what kind of an image are we reflecting? Like a mirror, we reflect an image which others can see. The image that God wants us to project is the image of himself. Our job as fathers is to reflect the Father to those around us.

The kind of image a mirror projects depends mostly on its direction and how clean its surface is. The task that faces us is to focus squarely on God and discover how to reflect his image to those we love. To do this we have to learn his perspective for the others in our lives. However, to discover God's focus we must first take an honest look at ourselves. What are our priorities now? Who is most important to us? Is our vision of life blurred? Can we see God's will in our lives? The answers to these questions can be painful, but they're the only place to begin.

If we're seeking God's direction, we can expect him to give it. He gave the Spirit to teach and lead us. The Holy Counselor will reveal the areas in a man's life which are in need of change: the blemishes on our reflecting surface. He will expose those areas in love, at a pace which we can stand. God wants to redeem us, not crush or condemn us. Once the areas needing change are clear, we can invite the Spirit to begin his work of redemption.

When we do this, we quickly discover that shifting priorities isn't so hard after all. We don't have to do it on our own power. In fact, we can't. A man can't change his life by the power of his own will. It's only the power of the Spirit that redeems life. The Holy Spirit reveals, convicts, and provides the power to change. The key to shifting priorities is knowing where the power comes from, or, to be more exact, *who* the power comes from. The power belongs to God. He will teach us how to use it.

Seeking the Truth

The deeper work of the Holy Spirit in us produces a hunger for truth. In Jesus, we find the perfect embodiment of truth. He has come to dispel the half-truths of the world, the flesh, and Satan—the father of lies. "Jesus then went on to say to those Jews who believed in him: 'If you live according to my teaching, you are truly my disciples; then you will know the truth, and the truth will set you free'" (Jn 8:31-32).

The truth is not just a set of principles; it is a living person—Jesus, the Son of God. He lived a human life on this earth, in real circumstances and worldly situations. Our encounter with the living person of Jesus immediately exposes a major stumbling block—pride, our human inheritance. A struggle goes on constantly within a Christian between our root sin of pride and the work of the Spirit of God as he reveals the full truth of Jesus. Our human pride is strong and it wants to be in control. It resists God's truth which can set us free. There is no question that the truth which Jesus brings will hurt our pride. The hurt will be there until we begin to experience the freedom promised to us as sons of God.

This sounds painful and it is, but God does not leave us in pain. The action of the Spirit is described as a two-edged sword. The leading edge of truth cuts into our old ways, but the final action of the Advocate is to console and to heal. As the process of reorienting our lives moves on, we come to see the ultimate action of God as restoration, not condemnation.

The truth of Jesus not only hurts our pride, but it exacts a price. The cost of freedom is that of being a disciple, a follower of the full gospel. As we begin to yield our old ideas to Jesus and accept a totally new way of living, the true freedom promised by Jesus becomes a reality for us.

When we invite Jesus more deeply into our hearts, we become more acutely aware of the untruth still present in all of us. It can be fairly shocking. This did not happen to me until about five years after I had made the Cursillo. This experience was my first encounter with the creative force of the unconditional love of God. For five years, my life changed—externally. It was during that gestation period that God's grace gently began to soak into the hard crust which had built up over thirty years.

During the early stages of renewal I made new friends, changed my activities, and started using a new language— "Christianese." These were welcome changes, but God wanted more. Slowly but surely, the Father established his position in my heart. When I was ready, he showed me the need for deeper redemption of my motives, attitudes, and thought patterns. The experience which brought conversion into these new areas was baptism in the Holy Spirit. To my surprise, I became aware that I had limited Jesus to the safer parts of my life. Now the Spirit was set free to probe the deeper areas.

When I allowed the Spirit to reveal a clearer picture of my true priorities, I discovered that I devoted far more time and energy to worldly achievement than to prayer, study, and loving action. A strong achievement orientation had been bred into me. My childhood during the Depression had created a deep need for security. The military training I later received strengthened my task orientation and fed my spirit of competition. The need to "be first" motivated me in business, and I became a very successful man of the world. That achievement, however, couldn't ease the pain I felt upon realizing my weakness as a husband and a father. I had been relying on Anna to care for the spirituality of our family.

As the light of the Spirit gradually dawned in me, the old compromises sounded hollow. The excuse that "I'm doing all this for my wife and children" didn't seem to justify missing dinner night after night for business meetings. The Spirit also showed me that I wasn't alone in this condition. I saw many other men—close friends and business associates—sacrificing wives, children, homes, health and even Jesus in order to climb a corporate ladder. Their careers occupied first place in their minds and hearts. Unfortunately, this is the motivation that drives many American men. For them, as it was for me, work is the priority. I had reached a painful awareness: Achievement and recognition, not a hunger for the Kingdom of God, had become the driving force which motivated my decisions and behavior. In essence, I was meeting God's plan with plain rebellion.

Renegade Males

This kind of rebellion causes endless unrest in our families. The root of it doesn't lie in society, our schools, or our Church, but in ourselves. It is the basic rebellion of sons against their father. We can be rebellious children even when we grow up and become fathers ourselves. Derek Prince, an internationally known Christian teacher, has phrased it this way: "The basic problem with America today is renegade males!"

Who do we blame for the absence of positive images of manhood in our society? Our wives? Women's lib? We might even say, "We live in a matriarchal society," until we look for a good definition of that word "matriarchal." R.J. Rushdooney, in his book The *Institutes of Biblical Law*, stated, "The trend toward a matriarchal society is in evidence in western culture today. It should be stressed that, contrary to popular opinion, a matriarchal society is not a society in which women rule, but rather a society in which men fail to exercise their dominion, so that women are faced with a double responsibility."

Let's face it. We are the problem! We fathers are the principal vehicle to bring God's grace into our families, yet in many instances we're not fully appropriating that grace. We are the most direct path of God's love to our wives and children, but many times we decide to block the path. We actually choose to resist God. I don't believe men do this consciously, but we're surrounded by ways of thinking, patterns of behavior, and spiritual forces which cloud the truth. Many of us have accepted the lie that, "This is the way it's always been" or "This is the way it has to be." God is merciful. However, he doesn't want our excuses or complaints. He wants men who will stand up and act like men. Brothers, let's not fight it any longer. We are the problem and God wants to do something about it.

The Lord's Balance

We can begin to answer God's call to become responsible fathers by recognizing that we can't change on our own. Jesus—the one who offers the full truth—must teach us how to restructure our lives according to God's plan. We begin by trying to integrate Jesus into our daily life.

One day while driving along thinking about this need to yield more fully to Jesus, I noticed two men jogging alongside the road. They looked like ordinary joggers, yet I noticed that they were in perfect step with one another. One man was following the other in complete unison. This was an image of that relationship of unity I needed to have with Jesus. He is the leader and the teacher; he walks before me. This is the first step in dealing with ourselves—to get in step with Jesus.

We get in step with Jesus by seeking a balanced life, one in which our decisions and behavior patterns are in line with God's priorities. It is a life centered on the basics—where loving actions flow out of a regular prayer life and a disciplined set of study habits. Here is a list of basic steps which I'm taking to balance my personal life:

1. Going before the Lord in prayer each day, regardless of how I feel.

2. Developing a regular life of worship, which includes the sacraments and shared prayer.
3. Disciplining myself through fasting.
4. Reading the scripture every day.
5. Developing a good spiritual study program.
6. Conforming my mind and my behavior to the Word of God.
7. Being alert to additional changes needed in my life.
8. Appropriating the power of God to follow through on change.

Each of these basic steps has to be at least underway if we are to live out the call to fatherhood. However, even a decision to take these steps doesn't automatically make them happen. They take time and effort. God doesn't ask for instant perfection, but he does insist on a sincere effort to bring our lives into balance. The effort which we put into these fundamentals must be *at least* as great as our efforts in the other areas such as work, education, recreation, and community service.

Planning for Change

My efforts to center my life on these fundamentals was a struggle until I decided to take advantage of some wisdom I had obtained through management training. The insight I used was this: "Plan your work and work your plan." I had become proficient in working out creative plans for my job, but I hadn't done so for the most important assignment of my life. Now I started applying some of those management tools to my spiritual and family life.

Using the principles of management by objective, I developed clear goals and objectives for my fatherhood and then worked out step-by-step plans to accomplish those objectives. Planning was fine except I had to reverse many of my management principles; most of them applied to situations where relationships were superficial and only tangible results were desired.

I had to realize that Christianity is a radical style of life, and the priorities and norms of the world are, in many instances, completely out of step with God. Getting into step with Jesus

ing stories which had next to nothing to do with my priorities as a Christian father. At first this decision appeared to reduce my awareness of what was happening in the world, but I soon realized that it is not necessary to have a daily paper to keep informed. My deeper need was to read scripture more, to get into closer touch with God's word. This choice freed a lot of time and energy to study the Bible and other life-giving reading material.

After newspapers, I started looking for other drains on my creative energy and found a large one sitting in our family room—the TV set. Television has its place but we've got to carefully regulate it to avoid being saturated with worldly formation. In our society—and in our homes—the television has become a primary source of formation for children, and unfortunately, for fathers and mothers too. If you think you don't have enough time to pray and study, look carefully into the number of hours you spend with TV and newspapers.

I discovered another misplaced priority right in the middle of my body: my stomach. For me overeating had become an artform. Too often my thoughts drifted toward snacks and how I could please my already oversized stomach. Christian fathers have to be men of discipline in their eating habits, as well as other areas. Fasting is a necessary part of our program of shifting priorities. You may not have an overeating problem, but there might be some other excess which needs to be curbed.

These are some specific areas which needed basic refocusing in my life. I'm sure you could add your own. Perhaps some would be the same as mine. Changes such as these recenter our lives on the Lord, and are the basis for larger changes later. The main point to remember is: pray first; *then* make a plan. Look at your life realistically and ask the Lord to reveal what needs changing. Decide to make little changes, working on one area at a time. You will find that this will become a continuous process and that the successful shifts will motivate you to keep going.

The concept of planning for change has led me to develop a family pastoral plan for making the shifts needed in our home. It is based on the idea of discovering the most critical change

requires decisions which may directly contradict our con[
tional human wisdom. The gospel challenges us with p
doxes. "Sell all you have and give it to the poor. You will [
treasure in heaven" (Lk 18:22). "Whoever would save his
will lose it, but whoever loses his life for my sake will fin[
(Mt 16:25).

Gospel wisdom calls for a new way. Here are some rule
planning your life in the Kingdom of God:

1. Place God first.
2. Take the last place for yourself.
3. Put your family between you and God.

The image that comes to me is that of a bow and arrow[
bow represents the power of God's Spirit to propel us to
the Kingdom. The arrow represents our family. While Go[
full authority over our lives, he has blessed us with freed[
choice. We fathers have a great deal to do with how fa[
the bow is drawn and in what direction the arrow is sho[
power comes from God but we must decide where and [
use it. The rule for fatherhood planning is: Take your
behind your family, ask God to draw back for ma[
power, and aim at the Kingdom.

Personal Decisions

I quickly learned that my decision to plan and act ir
dance with God's priorities had to begin with some sm[
crete decisions. We can get immobilized if we try to s[
focus in every area at once. Jesus wants us to do what
and leave the rest to him. So I began to make some sr
difficult changes.

One of the first was a decision to give up some of
and sleep time and use it for my highest priority—[
chose to pray more and sleep less in order to grow as
God. This involved taking small blocks of time when
relaxed or napped and devoting them to prayer. I c[
the focus of that time.

Another practical decision entailed cutting down [
papers. I discovered how much time and energy I sp[

needed at one time and developing a concrete plan to bring it about. A pastoral plan for any environment, especially for a Christian family, involves identifying needs and resources, then deciding how to bring them together.

In developing my family pastoral plan, I had to be realistic about my resources. None of us has the wisdom and grace to meet all of our family's needs. I had to go outside my immediate surroundings for help to pastor my family in new ways. The kind of resources which we have today—books, tapes, and experienced friends—were not readily available when I first realized my need. It was frustrating to sense a desire for something good but not know how quite to address it. However, I soon discovered that God doesn't call us to change without providing resources to accomplish it. The Father definitely equips us to complete any mission that he calls us to. The resources weren't at my fingertips, but with some prayer and searching, the answers started to appear.

The earliest help I received in defining and shifting my priorities came from other committed Christian families, near and far away. Slowly but surely we received what was needed to respond to God.

Look around you. The Lord has already given you an abundance of help. Read what is available, but also try to find one other person who has successfully made the change you want to make. If that person is willing to help you, do what he or she suggests.

Fathers should also draw on the resources right in their homes—in the form of wives and children. Listen and learn from them! Ask them to help you discover what God is saying. I had to learn to receive this day-to-day love and encouragement. When I accepted it, I learned another principle of Christian fatherhood: When God wants to speak powerfully to a man about an area of his fatherhood which needs adjustment, that word will usually come through the people who live with him and love him the most.

A few words of caution about trying to make changes in your lifestyle based on the advice or example of others: Be sure to adapt what you receive to your own situation, and don't try to change everything at once. That was the first warning I received from my friends, yet I did exactly the opposite. The result was frustration and resentment—not loving action. God wants a reasonable effort—not instant perfection. Pick one area for change and concentrate on that. The success we experience will motivate us to go on to another. This is why AA and Weight Watchers celebrate little victories one at a time instead of looking too far ahead. We can begin to deal with ourselves by taking the same approach.

My First Shifts

Shifting priorities means getting back to basics, but it also involves people. We must both *know* our order of priority in relationships and *act* on this knowledge. In other words, we must take positive action to make the people closest to us a priority.

The scriptures clearly tell us that God is our first priority. I acknowledged that by making a decision to pray regularly. But this decision in itself wasn't enough. When should I pray? How long? In what way? These details would express concretely how important God really was to me.

Since God is my top priority, he should have first place in my day. These first moments of the day have proved to be prime time for prayer. Had I experienced trouble with prayer in the morning, I would need to change my prayer time to a better part of the day.

My next priority is my wife Anna. The years of marriage have taught me that little things mean a lot to a woman. I've always wanted to operate in broad sweeping programs, without realizing that little gestures of love were important to Anna. After failing at attempts to become the perfect husband, I finally realized that change meant little decisions for life and love.

This principle became evident to me at a hectic time. My work was very busy, and required a good bit of traveling. When not out of town, I was leaving home early and coming home late. I had little or no loving contact with Anna during the day. Under these circumstances, how could I grow closer to her? I thought about quitting the job, but this was an instinctive sweeping solution. While I prayed about it, a new thought entered my mind, "Just call Anna each day." That idea was too simple to have come from me, so I assumed it came from God. It was worth a try. I placed a little sign on my desk and in my briefcase—"Call Anna today!" It turned out this was the gesture of love she needed most at that time. What God wants in most situations is much easier than we imagine. A man wants to move a mountain in one step, but God's way is slow and steady.

Next in order of priority were my children. My lack of development as a father had begun to weigh heavy on my heart. I hoped that God would give me a major revelation about my children and show me how to correct all the problems at once. Instead, as Elijah discovered, the Spirit spoke in gentle, soft tones. God elected to speak about my children in a strange but very effective way. The channel he chose was my work—the real priority of my life at that time. It was the place where I was already most attentive.

The Lord spoke when Anna and I were attending an industry convention in Atlanta. The speaker at one of the sessions was discussing leadership in business. He said something very simple, "If you want to lead people, you must be *physical* and *visible* to them." These words stirred my heart. They were God's words for my fatherhood. Our children needed my presence—a physical and visible father. I eventually acted on that word, and shifted my schedule to allow me to be home as much as possible. From that point, many other changes occurred, but all have flowed from an initial decision to be present and visible to my children. I didn't have to fully understand God's word—I had to be obedient.

These first shifts in priority have opened my heart and mind for greater changes. Each new awareness has shown that God was asking for things I could do, not the impossible which would only frustrate me. I had to let the Lord lead me at his pace. Three feasible, concrete changes came first: prime time for prayer, reaching out to Anna each day, and being physical and visible at home. Those decisions have been the basis of everything else. They can be for you too.

Reevaluating Priorities

We must be attentive to the Spirit's leading as we grow in maturity as fathers. The Lord does not want us to rest on past success. He wants us to continually reevaluate our priorities and allow him to show us what needs to change next.

A good tool to use as we grow in fatherhood is what I would call the Spotlight Principle. I learned it as the manager of a business. The manager surveys many departments: sales, operations, bookkeeping, collections, finance, service, etc. The mature executive knows that every department is at a different stage of efficiency. His job is to manage change, so he concentrates on the area which is in the most need. He then turns to another department, and then to the next. As the manager develops his skills, he learns to keep the spotlight of his attention moving at just the right pace, so that each area is given the help it needs to keep improving. The manager is interested in the overall activity; he is not especially concerned about a temporary slip in one area or another. We can apply this perspective to the task of managing our priorities. We are concerned with the overall reordering of our lives into the model of Jesus. We can use the Spotlight Principle to avoid crisis management, where our lives are being controlled by our circumstances.

Sometimes the spotlight of God's Spirit will shine on some elusive problems. We can usually detect misdirected time and energy in our secular situations, but as we shift into spiritual commitments, we can fall into a subtle trap. Just because a situation is spiritual, we can immediately think it's part of God's plan for us. This is not necessarily true. We must constantly reevaluate our priorities in light of God's word for us *now*. After many years of working in church renewal activities, I have learned that these commitments can get as imbalanced as anything else. We can't assume that each ministry or service we're asked to perform is right for us. Seek the Lord's will for every decision, and don't be afraid to say, "no." In my own life, I've grown as a father at least as much by saying no, as I have by saying yes.

We also need to know when to stop doing something. A service or apostolate which was right six months or six years ago may not be where God wants us now. We can delude ourselves just as thoroughly working in the Kingdom of God as we can in the world. We can sincerely believe that we are indispensable and that things will collapse if we pull back. If that's true—pull back fast. Only God is indispensable. By clutching to some current activity, we could be preventing God from doing something new for us.

One last point about shifting priorities: God will elect to use crisis to change us if he has to. This is not his first plan, but we can find ourselves in situations which need rapid, decisive action. During a crisis, the energy levels are way up, and amazing changes can occur. Don't be afraid of these times; the Lord is always in control and he will never leave us alone. When God wants a major change in our lives, he will tolerate a temporary imbalance in our normal priorities. As we respond to his will, the situation will settle down. Then it is time to refocus and get our priorities back in order.

Remember, the key to shifting priorities is knowing that the power comes from God. The transmission of a car is a good analogy. The power to move the car and to change its direction lies in the engine. But unless that power is transmitted to the wheels, nothing happens. The engine just runs. We need to be in the right gear, like that transmission. Shifting priorities means getting God's power in gear and moving in the direction he wants. The power is there, but we must choose to engage it.

A Christian father begins to change by first discovering what his actual priorities are and then asking God to help him to reorder them. The fruits of this loving action are peace, joy, and love, grown from seeds which were sown in the field of the Spirit.

CHAPTER FIVE

Prayer:
A Personal Discipline

A "prayer explosion" seems to be going on today. Workshops on prayer, reflection, meditation are frequent and crowded. Transcendental Meditation becomes a mass movement. Eastern religions emphasizing the need for contemplation are becoming quite popular. There is even a move afoot to bring prayer back into the classroom. Why is this happening?

At the bottom of it is a search for truth. We have found the pace of modern life both exhausting and shallow. Man is saying, "There must be something more to life than working, eating, sleeping, and dying." The quest for meaning in life has always driven man toward God. That is what is happening today as man realizes the answers to his questions are beyond human wisdom.

A new interest in prayer is also visible among Christians. Men and women who have been engaged in church activities are now also hungry for a deepening of their personal relationship with God. They are no longer satisfied with new liturgy, new theology, and the slogan, "My work is my prayer." Even the intellectual and the theologian who may have been content with knowledge about God now want to *know him* not know about him.

In his book *Prayer is a Hunger*, Fr. Edward Farrell put it well: "As man reaches out to the stars and touches ever expanding space, he is drawn to the discovery and value of his inner space. Prayer no longer lies on the edge of life. It moves into the core of the person's life and meaning. Without prayer, there is no way, no truth, no life."

For many Christians, the desire for prayer has been unsatisfied. They ask, "Why am I still feeling confused?" When I encounter a mature Christian who is confused or frustrated I usually begin with a simple question: "How's your prayer life?" Most of us will look for complicated reasons to explain our confusion. The root of our problem is often much simpler: a lack of discipline and the absence of regular personal prayer.

The most important of the many forms of prayer and worship is daily private dialogue with the Father. This chapter will focus mainly on this kind of prayer, and the struggles which we all have with it. Christians have received the gift of the Holy Spirit to "teach us all things." The deepest truths in Christianity are available to every believer as we decide to pray directly and personally to God. We have no elite class of Christians. The Kingdom is open to us all—in prayer.

Prayer—A Must

Prayer is not something we do for God. It is something God does through the Spirit who dwells within us. It is through the action of God that our relationship with him grows. The Father must have time to teach us who we really are as sons of God. Our identity in the Kingdom begins to unfold as we become men of prayer. A man must know "who he is" and only his father can explain that to him.

Prayer is also essential if we are to serve God rightly. Too often we try to serve him in the wrong ways and with the wrong motives. We need to see our service from God's perspective, as a joy and not drudgery. The attitude of willing service is nurtured in prayer. Our service for God makes little sense unless we understand his mind about it.

We also need a rich prayer life if we are to experience some form of community or shared life. Efforts to form community without a firm grounding in the discipline of personal prayer usually fail. Meaningful shared life can only flow from shared prayer among individuals who are experiencing a deep personal union with God.

Prayer is critical if we are to have something of value for others. We cannot rely just on our gifts, resources, and ideas. Those around us need to receive God's word through us. They will not receive it unless we seek that word in prayer.

Personal prayer is essential for renewed corporate prayer. When our liturgy and other worship services seem to be dull, the solution is not to be found just in renewed rites, but also in the renewal of personal piety.

For Christian fathers, prayer is absolutely central. Fatherhood is difficult without the revelation and direction which comes through prayer. God wants to unfold his plan for our lives and our families; we need to take the time to listen to him. Could you imagine trying to train one of your children if he wouldn't sit still and listen to your instruction? We must *decide* to sit and be taught by God. Otherwise we will stumble around in confusion and darkness. As we grow in relationship with the Father through our prayer, we can be taught everything we need to know. The wisdom we need to shepherd our flocks is provided freely to a man who seeks.

I realized how freely the Spirit had taught me only when I began to write this book. I spent days and weeks going through my personal journals and found that God had taught me in prayer most of what I had to know. I later did research to give a solid base to my work. This was a joy because it simply confirmed what God had already revealed. I have been frankly amazed at how much we are taught through diligent listening to God.

We need personal union with the Father in prayer to expand our vision. We don't understand the power and the grace of fatherhood; so God must explain it to us. He must broaden our horizons and show us our place in his plan. Consider how God dealt with Abraham, our father in faith.

"When Abram was ninety-nine years old, the Lord appeared to him and said: 'I am God the Almighty. Walk in my presence and be blameless. Between you and me I will establish my covenant, and I will multiply you exceedingly.' When Abram prostrated himself, God continued to speak to him: 'My covenant with you is this: you are to become the father of a host of nations'" (Gn 17:1-4).

Imagine yourself childless at ninety-nine. Would you have a vision of fatherhood? God gave Abram a vision beyond his wildest imagination: he became the father of a nation, and God worked a miracle of life and salvation for all men through his obedient heart. God wants to work miracles; he needs men who will agree to be his instruments.

A Daily Discipline

To learn about prayer, we should look to the example of Jesus. He prayed to establish communion with the Father and to provide strength for a full immersion into life, not an escape from it. His is the perfect example for the Christian man who must draw courage and vision in prayer to live the gospel in his everyday life. Jesus' public ministry drained him as our work drains us; the source of his replenishment is the same as ours. I would like to highlight just a few characteristics of the prayer of Jesus which can serve as inspiration and instruction for us.

The prayer of Jesus is *simple and to the point*. "In your prayer do not rattle on like the pagans. They think they will win a hearing by the sheer multiplication of words. Do not imitate them. Your Father knows what you need before you ask him" (Mt 6:7-8).

The man of prayer must find the *right place and the right time* to be alone with God. "Rising early the next morning, he went off to a lonely place in the desert; there he was absorbed in prayer" (Mk 1:35). "Whenever you pray, go to your room, close your door, and pray to your Father in private" (Mt 6:6). "Then he went out to the mountain to pray, spending the night in communion with God" (Lk 6:12).

Our prayer must be *honest*. "Then Jesus went to a place called Gethsemani....He said to them [his followers], 'My heart is nearly broken with sorrow. Remain here and stay awake with me.' He advanced a little and fell prostrate in prayer. 'My Father, if it is possible, let this cup pass me by'" (Mt 26:36, 38, 39).

The prayer of *forgiveness and abandonment* is always heard by the Father. "When they came to Skull Place, as it was called, they crucified him there....Jesus said, 'Father, forgive them; they do not know what they are doing.' ...It was now around midday and darkness came over the whole land....Jesus uttered a loud cry and said, 'Father, into your hands I commend my spirit.' After he said this he expired" (Lk 23:33, 34, 44, 46).

By the example of his life, his words, and his prayer, Jesus taught simple men how to relate to God and each other. He spent time, even through the night, to gain the wisdom and power he needed to serve the Father and the people of God. He taught his followers to be men of prayer. He did not leave us with a list of formal prayers, but rather with the example of a life spent in prayer.

Throughout Church history, Christians have followed Jesus' example. The apostle Paul called for constant prayer. "Rejoice always, never cease praying, render constant thanks; such is God's will for you in Christ Jesus" (1 Thes 5:16-17). The prayer life of the Church is constant; we are called to join with that, in some way. For me, the experience of praying at regular intervals during the day has become a real treat. All of us can "rejoice always" by stopping periodically to renew our communion with the Father. "No matter where we happen to be, by prayer we can set up an altar to God in our heart" (St. John Chrysostom).

A technique which can help us pray constantly is the "Jesus prayer," one of the earliest prayer forms of the Christian church. The Jesus prayer has its origins among the early Christians and the monastic orders. Its shortest form has two parts: First, "Lord Jesus Christ;" the second, "have mercy on me." Simply repeating and meditating on the meaning of those seven words can draw us closer to God and strengthen our daily relationship with him. The Jesus prayer illustrates a principle: As we become more disciplined in prayer, we should be able to pray in simpler and more direct ways.

Developing this kind of daily discipline will help us avoid the pitfall of praying only when we need something. God does not want our prayer to be crisis-oriented, but a regular part of our day. I think it is also true that regular prayer-like good habits of eating, rest, and exercise—will help us physically and emotionally as well as spiritually. Let me tell you about one man who fit this description.

A few years ago I had the opportunity to witness Archbishop Fulton J. Sheen in action. Our local church had been able to engage Bishop Sheen as a speaker for an anniversary celebration. The man at that time was in his late seventies. I hadn't seen him since the early days of television when our entire family would gather to enjoy his weekly show.

There was an air of excitement as the crowd waited for our famous guest. I was expecting a wise, but a somewhat frail elderly man. Much to my surprise Bishop Sheen turned out to be a healthy, vigorous man of God who didn't look much different than he did twenty-five years earlier. He walked jauntily through the crowd after driving from the airport and spoke for more than an hour without any evident signs of fatigue. Apparently others were just as amazed at his vitality, and someone asked what his secret was. He replied, "I spend at least one hour in prayer every morning before the Blessed Sacrament." The bishop commented that when he sees sad and unhappy Christians, he knows that they haven't been listening to God.

The witness of a prayerful, disciplined life is not meant to be confined to cloistered religious and powerful preachers like Bishop Sheen. The power of the Spirit which filled these holy men is just as available to the working father whose life also needs that vigor. The secret of prayer is discipline and decision.

How to Pray

My wife Anna tells a favorite story which could introduce any discussion about how to pray. She says that during the 1950s many young monks would gather around Thomas Merton, the famous mystical writer, and ask him to teach them about prayer. Merton's response was wise. He said, "If you want to learn how to pray, pray!"

Our prayer is a conversation with God. It is the fruit of an established relationship which God has initiated and in which we have cooperated. Since none of us has seen God, we must use inadequate models to describe this expression of the relationship between God and man. However, since God is our father and since he has made us sons, the best model for our relationship is that of a conversation between a loving human father and his natural child. Our God is a *personal* God.

When I sit down to talk with one of my children, I expect that we both will be very conscious of the presence of the other person. We are both very aware of each other. We look into each other's eyes and sit down to begin a two-way conversation. Usually I'll initiate the conversation myself.

Beginning to pray demands the recognition that we are not alone and that the God who is present wants to love and encourage us. Prayer can begin when we can think of God in a "you and I" context. This acknowledgement of the personal presence of God in our hearts is where we open our conversation. No block should separate us. If repentance is needed, this is a good place to begin.

The simple awareness of God's personal nature is one of those truths which have been "revealed to the merest of children." It is a truth which can elude the proud man who wants to deal with God as an equal, not as a child. A classic and well-known example of this is Albert Einstein's lifelong struggle to accept the existence of God and fit him into the theories of matter, energy, and relativity. Einstein was finally able to acknowledge a "supreme force," but the awareness of a personal God eluded him. Despite his genius, Einstein missed the elementary truth that only a personal God could create persons. We can't relate to God intellectually; we must meet him as a personal fatherly presence, waiting to sit and talk with us.

From my experience in attempting to grow in prayer, I have concluded that the time and place we choose are also very important. If I wanted to speak intimately to my son, I wouldn't pick the family living room at 5:30 p.m. or a car on a crowded expressway. I would find a quiet private place where my son could feel free to sit in my lap if he wanted to and express whatever thought or emotion he desired. I'd also choose a time when we were physically relaxed and mentally alert.

You should ask the Lord's guidance about the best time and place to pray. Also, don't be afraid to experiment with new times and places. You'll know you've found the right combination when your prayer can begin without excess distraction, either within you or externally. When you find the best place and time, stick with it until the Lord leads you to change. A pattern of prayer is best supported by familiar surroundings which are associated with fruitful times spent in God's presence before.

Once we become aware of the personal presence of God, the next step is *praise*. "Pray perseveringly, be attentive to prayer, and pray in a spirit of thanksgiving" (Col 4:2). Praise is the creature's most natural expression of thanks to his creator. Praise is also a spiritual weapon to fight distraction, confusion, and exhaustion. "Out of the mouths of babes and sucklings, you have fashioned praise because of your foes, to silence the hostile and the vengeful" (Ps 8:3). The greeting of praise, especially that which is expressed through charismatic gifts of the Spirit, sets our childlike stance in clear contrast to the awesomeness of God. Our thanksgiving for the blessings of life and love can be a personal litany of praise. Also, we may want to seed our praise by using the words of the Psalms or other scriptures written to lift thanks to the Lord.

The Jews were an earthy and wholesome people who understood the magnitude of the Almighty and our difficulty relating to him in any way except childlike gestures. Hebrew provides a broader equivalent to our English word "prayer." For them worship meant actions of praise; songs, shouts, dance, jumping and so forth. They did not pray passively. When a child sees his father after being separated for a while, he leaps into his arms and shouts for joy.

This opening time of praise should be one when we can freely express ourselves. If you are so inclined, find a place where you can shout, sing, leap, or dance. It's difficult to move into the later stages of prayer if we don't let the child in us have a time to rejoice and be free in the presence of his Father.

For many men, the freedom to be childlike is realized as their conversion experience progresses. Before that, just the thought of touching another human being was frightening. Their personal encounter with Jesus puts this fear to death, awakening healthy emotions toward others and new expressions of love for God. However, others may still be struggling to overcome inhibition about expressing praise with their bodies. Although the Father is pleased with any attempt at prayer, we can hope for a renewed freedom in praise. If you can shout for your favorite sports team, you can shout and leap before God.

The actual conversational dialogue between father and son begins after they are aware of each other's presence and when they have embraced and greeted each other in praise and thanksgiving for the love they share. A conversation is usually begun by the one who has invited the other. When one of my children says, "Dad, could we sit down and talk a little?" I expect that he will begin the discussion. Similarly, we must expect to open the dialogue with God. This could be a lofty explanation of the condition of your life or a plea for help that day, but it must always be a true reflection of what you want to say. God knows the deepest part of your heart, so don't waste time with fine-sounding phrases. When one of my children begins this way, I know he's trying to cover up something and I must wait until he's ready to say what he's really thinking. You won't shock God! Tell him what's on your mind and don't use double talk.

After we've spoken to God, it's time to *listen* to our Father speak. Communication with God in prayer has more to do with our capacity to listen than with our ability to speak. The Lord, like a loving Father, has been patiently waiting for us to stop so he can begin to speak in the way he has chosen to respond.

This part of our prayer is the most important for our success in fatherhood. It's the time when we are fathered by God, receiving his perspective about our lives. We can expect an abundance of love and encouragement along with any necessary correction, but we must stop talking in order to hear what God has to say.

The voice of the Lord is heard in our hearts.

Consider what you would do if the president of your company asked you to be available for his call at 9:00 a.m. each morning. You would probably be at the phone long before that time. When the call came, you'd be ready to say, "Yes, sir, good morning, what should I do today?" If God was calling, we would receive his call even more eagerly. We would not waste precious time complaining. Actually, God is ready and available to us at any time, all we must do is invite him into our prayer and listen to him.

My personal prayer life has been evolving in cycles and periods. There are times when I can feel the electricity of God's presence and other times when it's very calm and ordinary. I've come to see the value in both times and I no longer try to gauge the quality of my prayer by my feelings. All my efforts at prayer bring me closer to God.

Nevertheless, I have learned things about prayer over the years. Certain directions seem to be evolving. A simplicity is replacing the complex methods I once relied on. Spiritual phrases are giving way to plain everyday language.

I'm also discovering that hearing God has a lot to do with asking him the right questions. I try not to ask difficult or abstract questions, but to speak about my true desires and concerns about my family. Usually, the leading of the Spirit on these matters is not difficult to discern. When Solomon prayed for wisdom and understanding so that he could lead God's people justly and prudently, the Lord was pleased and he responded quickly.

The times of my deepest contact with the Father are beginning to occur at odd hours, when everyone is asleep and the house is perfectly quiet. I can now understand why Jesus would go off and pray late at night or in the early morning. When I've got a knotty problem to untangle, I will usually ask the Lord to give me a little rest and then wake me up during the quiet of the night. If I'm ready to hear what he has to say, this will usually happen. The night is a good time to pray, but don't try it unless you're rested enough to miss the sleep and still be effective the next day.

A father who prays regularly is also a good example for his children. I used to become embarrassed when a child found me in prayer, but today I welcome it. How many of us have ever seen our fathers in prayer? This is the quiet witness which builds a child's image of a whole and holy man. Today, when I'm edgy or out of sorts, our children may ask, "Dad, have you prayed today?" They can see the difference.

Our Posture in Prayer

An important part of our listening to God has to do with our posture before him. I don't mean just our physical stance, although this is important; I'm referring to our inner openness to receive his word. Recall God's dialogue with Abram discussed earlier; the essence of his word was spoken after Abram prostrated himself before the Lord. This posture of genuine receptivity is what God is looking for in his children.

"When you call me, when you go to pray to me, I will listen to you. When you look for me, you will find me. Yes when you seek me with all your heart, you will find me with you" (Jer 29:12-13). God spoke these words through the prophet Jeremiah to his rebellious children Israel, then in exile in Babylon. The repetition of "when" emphasizes the conditional nature of God's promises. We must seek God with a humble and sincere heart if we expect to be able to receive his word to us. Jesus emphasized God's call to a receptive posture: "Take my yoke upon your shoulders and learn from me, for I am gentle and humble of heart" (Mt 11:29). A father whose spirit is prostrate before God will be in a position to be loved and directed by the Spirit.

The next part of the posture of prayer is coming to rest. We cannot hear the gentle quality in the voice of God if we do not take the time to be still.

A man who says he has no time to pray is as foolish as one who refuses to take a lunch break or get enough sleep; eventually his hectic pace burns him out. For most of us, the pace of modern life makes the quiet and peace needed for effective prayer almost impossible to attain. This can be a good excuse but it is not a valid reason to avoid doing whatever we can to change the pace of our lives.

Prayer demands our full attention; we can't do something else at the same time. Praying while driving or between meetings is helpful, but it is not the prayer that will produce a deep union with our Father. We must decide to stop, sit, and allow God to teach us.

After deciding to listen to God and have him direct my life, I had to acquire some new habits for my prayer. It seems that there are only two times when I can go into any depth in prayer; the first thing in the morning or during the night, after a minimum time of rest. I use my mornings for the normal listening and an occasional night time session for seeking answers which have continually eluded me. If I let the day's program of events or the mental backlog we all carry begin to invade my mind, it is very difficult to pray, my best time is when I am the most rested and not distracted. I also pray in short periods during the day, but effective listening is limited to time alone in a quiet and peaceful place.

If this style of prayer sounds mystical to you, that is what I am suggesting. We should be moving toward becoming modern-day mystics: men who have learned how to sense the presence of God and can distinguish his voice from the thousands of other voices in the world. For today's father, the life of deeper prayer can refresh and build us. The inner voice of the Spirit will tell us the Lord's perspective on our lives.

Overcoming Obstacles

Before there can be any growth in life, there is usually a bridge to cross. For me, the bridge to deeper prayer is fear. I have had to cross over many fears to draw closer to the Father.

The biggest fear is that caused by our false images of God. If we come from a childhood which was not grounded in selfless parental love, or if we have experienced deep personal hurts, we might fear risking deeper love, even with God.

The healing action of the Church, exercised through the sacraments and personal ministry, can address these fears and shed God's light on our false images. Whenever we recognize distortions, we should seek healing for them. The true image of God is Jesus. As we come to discover him through the many sources of revelation, the images of God which we create for ourselves, or which have been imposed on us, will begin to fade and be replaced by truth. Jesus has revealed God as "Abba," loving Father. We can depend on that.

In addition to false images of God, we can harbor fears of what God might ask of us. We can delude ourselves into thinking that God will require more than we are able to give. This is a lie which Satan, the father of lies, tells us. The truth is that God will never ask us to do or give more than he has prepared us for. The call from the Father leads to abundant life, not a fearful existence. "God is for us" (Rom 8:31).

Another hindrance to our ability to listen is a fear that we will not hear anything. The concern that God will not speak is also a distortion of the Adversary. A loving father would not turn his back on his son. A God who would go through the Cross to free us is not hard to reach. He is very available and hungry to speak. When communication breaks down, we must look to ourselves for the explanation.

Our next obstacle after fear is the *condition of our hearts.* Are we living in sin? If we are, the path to God in prayer is blocked. Repentance and reconciliation are needed. For many men, the obstacle of a broken relationship seems too small to confess; they're looking for bigger sins. However, the true nature of sin is a falling short in relationship. Take this seriously and repent of even that sin which seems small.

God is looking for humble sinners who want to turn around from pride and come toward him for mercy and love. "My sacrifice, O God, is a contrite spirit; a heart contrite and humbled, O God, you will not spurn" (Ps 51:19).

An obstacle which we all face is the one which Jesus wanted most to destroy: *self-centeredness.* A man who is usually thinking about himself, his job, his figure, his clothes, or other involvements with self, cannot become empty enough to pray. To communicate with God we must be open channels, freed of the distractions and worries which pull us back into ourselves.

Through effective prayer, the areas which are legitimate responsibilities can be viewed in God's perspective, rather than demanding too much of our thoughts and energy.

A remedy for this obstacle is fasting. It forces us to empty ourselves. Jesus himself prescribed fasting as the personal discipline for his apostles, especially when they came up against strong spiritual opposition. However, Jesus always linked fasting with prayer. Fasting without prayer is useless for our growth as spiritual fathers. It becomes an external sacrifice without the internal turning to God. This is the stimulation which brings us into deeper contact with the God who already dwells in us. The Catholic Church confirms this direction by continuing to require a limited fast before the Eucharist.

Fasting is essentially self-denial. While fasting usually means a purposeful "no" to food for a definite period of time, it can also involve other forms of self-denial. The men I know who have grown in their prayer lives have invariably used fasting and other forms of discipline to overcome the obstacle of self-centeredness. They are essential, not optional, to a life of personal union with God and effective service to God's people.

An obstacle which Jesus warned against is *distraction*. "Enough, then, of worrying about tomorrow. Let tomorrow take care of itself. Today has troubles enough of its own" (Mt 6:34). We carry a pile of mental concerns, some real and others imagined, into our time with God. We can spend most of our allotted time of prayer trying to sort through these distractions and never get to what God wanted us to hear. The best attack on this problem which I have found has been to write my prayers.

This idea was offered to me by an old friend who made a habit of stopping at a park on his way to work, writing down his prayers in the quiet of a natural setting, and then meditating on what God had said. He convinced me that written prayers would reduce my tendency to become distracted by floating thoughts and would also help me get down to the essence of prayer quicker.

This technique has worked well at certain times of my life, not always. Writing what I am thinking forces me to be concise, and usually more honest. This style of prayer has led me to begin a spiritual journal which I've maintained in recent years. Looking back over my journal, I can see how God has acted in my life. It reduces my tendency to get discouraged and proves to me that the dry periods in prayer do not last forever.

As we write our prayer and our sense of God's response, we create our personal record of faith. This is the most valuable gift which we can give to our children—a lasting remembrance of their spiritual heritage. It will tell them what we have experienced and come to believe. What greater gift can we leave them to carry for their journey through life?

CHAPTER SIX

Study:
Forming Our Minds

Not long ago, I heard an interview with James Michener, the famous novelist, on a local radio show. As a writer myself, I was interested in his thoughts and opinions, especially when Michener was asked how many ideas in his books were original. He answered "very few," saying that in his entire life he had had only a few original thoughts. Michener had succeeded as a writer through diligent research and study of the subject he was writing about.

The same is true for fathers. As with any calling in life, growth in fatherhood is accompanied by an ongoing program of study. To succeed in the most important assignment of our lives, we must submit our minds to a process of Christian formation. This need is lifelong; it does not disappear once we have achieved a particular level of expertise. With progress, we realize how much more there is to know.

"Ideals," the first talk on my Cursillo weekend, introduced me to the need for study. I was told that we humans are rational beings with an irresistible desire to be like God. We are integrated beings: body, mind, and spirit. The Father has made us higher than the animal world by giving us the capacity to think. At the same time we are not pure spirit and never will be. God created angels with intellects not tied to a material body; therefore, he completely infused knowledge into them at their creation. Man is not so destined; he must acquire his knowledge bit by bit. The information and experiences which we collect in our minds are essential for judgment and decision-making. Thus the quality of the intellectual material we absorb is crucial to our well-being.

In a sense, the mind is analogous to our bodies. Both take in food. If we eat good, wholesome, nutritious food, our bodies will be healthy. The same is true of the mind. If we take in proper mental food, this faculty will be well formed. Our minds, like our bodies, assimilate and become what we feed them.

A Christian father's mind must be formed by a disciplined exposure to God's revelation, brought to him through the written word of the Scriptures and the living word of the Church. After prayer, a good program of regular study is our most important personal discipline. We must know what is involved in being the spiritual leader of a family.

Our Need for Knowledge

Study and the knowledge it yields is an integral part of our personal relationship with God. We cannot be satisfied with a concept of God which seems comfortable. To *know* God means to develop a full relationship with him. Applying our minds provides substance for our prayer to digest.

Study is essential because of the kind of beings we are. If we were purely spiritual beings, we could develop a mystical relationship with God which would mean that our communication with the Father could be beyond our minds. Conversely if we were simply a material creation, natural religion would suffice. However, we are also intellectual beings. The prayer of modern man must contain a stirring on all three levels: body, mind, and spirit.

Study can be looked upon as loving God with our minds. It is the willful submission of this critical part of our being to the Lordship of Jesus. Our mind, like the rest of us, must be redeemed by God's grace. We can allow the Spirit to change the way we think and thereby influence the way we pray.

Study is different from prayer, but it directly influences one's ability to pray. As we grow in the knowledge of God, we are more inclined to pray. Through the discipline of Christian study, we make our union with God a conscious one. We become more aware of just how God is our Father, Jesus is our brother, and the Holy Spirit is our intimate counselor. We can then pray more freely, since God's truth is present in our consciousness.

Prayer and study lead to loving action—the third part of our basic relationship with God. In the end, we will be held responsible for how we act. The knowledge, thoughts, hopes, feelings, and other unseen parts of our beings will be judged only insofar as they motivate actions. A Christian father will be judged on how well he imitates and reflects the loving actions of God to his family. To do so, he must form his responses through prayer and study.

Formation of the Christian Mind

There are three essential sources for the formation of a Christian mind: familiarity with God's word, discernment of our social and cultural environments, and meditation on the natural creation.

Scripture

The first and most important of these sources is the Word of God—the Holy Scriptures of the Old and New Testaments.

A useful Catholic work which has helped many to understand God's revelation in the Bible is the *Jerome Biblical Commentary*. This fine work begins with a statement from the *Dei Verbum*—the Vatican II document on scripture. Here is an excellent expression of the importance of scripture to the Christian:

> In the sacred books the Father who is in heaven meets his children with great love and speaks with them; and the force and power in the Word of God is so great that it remains the support and energy of the Church, the strength of faith for her sons, the food of the soul, the pure and perennial source of spiritual life.

Study of the scriptures is not an option for a Christian father; it is essential. Our principal source for wisdom and truth is the revelation of God's will and his perspective as contained in the Bible. Fathers who are not grounded in the Word will not achieve the success which God wants for them. The Hebrew prophets regarded scripture as essential, as something directly linked to the welfare of God's people. Hosea lamented, "My people perish for want of knowledge! Since you have rejected knowledge, I will reject you from my priesthood; since you ignored the law of your God, I will also ignore your sons" (Hos 4:6). The prophet Isaiah echoed the warning: "Therefore my people go into exile, because they do not understand" (Is 5:13). The words of the Jewish prophets were heard but not heeded. We can fall into the same trap. We can approach the Scriptures for entertainment or aesthetic value, and fail to base our lives on the word of God as the Father desires.

My own experience—and that of millions of other Christians—has been that the work of the Spirit in the life of a believer inspires a hunger for scripture and an ever-deepening knowledge of Jesus. As I went deeper into relationship with God and asked for the fullness of the Spirit to be released, my appetite for the Word grew. There are other sources of revelation, but the Bible is the most important. It is also the place to begin.

Another source available to us is the Church, the *living word* of God. The teachings of the Church and its tradition show us how to apply and interpret God's written word in our time. Since the scriptures are a reflection of a faith community on their experience of God, we continue to see God's action unfold our understanding of him today. "I, Wisdom, dwell with experience, and judicious knowledge I attain" (Prv 8:12).

My writing has provided me with the opportunity to read many documents of the Catholic Church which I previously had not been exposed to. I am amazed at the accuracy of perception given by the Holy Spirit to those in teaching authority. Although the complete implementation of Church teaching is always in process, the needs of God's people are seldom missed within the heart of the Church. Regardless of our denomination, Church teaching should be an integral part of our formation.

In addition to printed teaching we perceive revelation through the living ministry of ordained clergymen, religious, and committed laymen. This comes to us in almost overpowering dimensions today through the assistance of the media. The gift of anointed preaching of the word is alive in the Church, although not always immediately available to us. Even where the local preaching gifts are marginal, God seems to be providing other sources of stirring for our faith. Ministers who will preach God's word and inspired speakers in the renewal movements are gifts of the Father and should not be taken for granted.

Along with the written and living word, we can expect direct revelation of the Lord's plan for us as we grow in our relationship with Jesus and with other committed believers. For me, this has taken the form of personal prophecy and a sense of vision. The father of a family, like a shepherd, must be looking for the best place to lead his family. Although we can rejoice in prophecy as a public gift for ourselves and others, we must also cultivate a source of personal revelation and vision.

As we grow in union with God, we should ask him the questions that are most important to us as fathers. Where is the Spirit leading me? What does he want for my family? How are my children being called? Where are we called to serve in the Kingdom? We must ask the Lord to unfold his vision for us personally and as a family. He will answer, by revealing his particular plan for our lives. We can't lead our family on a borrowed vision; we must discover our own.

We will not receive this gift of prophetic vision without a spiritual transformation to match our deeper understanding. God wants sons who are willing to have their hearts and minds changed, in response to his words. "The Lord your God will circumcise your hearts and the hearts of your descendants, that you may love the Lord, your God, with all your heart and all your soul (mind), and so you may live" (Dt 30:6). The circumcision of the heart is the spiritual transformation God calls for.

Our Environments

The second essential source used in forming a Christian mind is our *environments*—the people, ideas, and circumstances which surround us. The gospel of Jesus is not just intended for personal conversion, but also to transform environments. We are called to participate in that process by first being sensitive to the spiritual climate of the environments in which we live, and further, by actively participating in the Spirit's work of transformation. The environments we live in make up our "sphere of influence." They include the people who surround us and the goals and drives which motivate them.

It is crucial to have good discernment about our environments, because they greatly affect our personal direction. If we are surrounded by people and ideas which support our Christian values, we will grow deeper in relationship with God. If the life around us does not support those values, we will have a difficult time. In short, our environments can either bring us closer to Jesus or drive a wedge between us and him. There is no "neutral" situation.

We should be cautious regarding environments, but not timid. The witness of living faith must go out to all we meet. As we deepen in our commitment to the Gospel we begin to see encounters with people as opportunities, not burdens. The best example I have had for this kind of openness to people has come from my good friend and spiritual advisor, Bishop Edward Hughes. Bishop Hughes makes it a habit to welcome all kinds of people into his life. He has said to me, "I expect to learn something from every person I meet." Those are the words of a humble man, who can see past the exterior classification of men into their hearts and minds, where Christ dwells. Those who enter his life are viewed as gifts from God, and welcomed as a resource for personal growth.

The discernment of our environments must begin with an honest look at ourselves. It was Plato who said, "Know thyself." What are our natural gifts? What experiences bring us joy? What temptations should we avoid? What is our heart's desire? A man who truly knows himself is aware of the strengths and weaknesses in his personality. He will not put himself in situations which will cause him serious temptation. He will be able to evaluate spiritual and material opportunities in light of truth, not personal fantasy.

Our environments also include definable groups such as communities, relationship groupings, service clubs, sports and recreation gatherings, and perhaps occupation and professional associations. These groups can both help and hinder our walk with the Lord. As my commitment to Christ and my family grew, I found it necessary to change many of the groups that were part of my life. These groups take time, and they greatly influence our values and our mind. We should be selective, and choose the right mix of groups—large and small, spiritual and secular—which we will be part of. We should be looking for depth in relationship, not just acquaintances.

Our environments should provide us with wisdom. We can get knowledge from many sources, but we only receive wisdom from God and those instruments of experience which he chooses to send to us. Next to God, the greatest source of wisdom for a Christian father is other Christian fathers. He should seek out such men, and spend time with them.

The task of finding the right set of environments for our Christian life is not easy. There is an abundant supply of human wisdom to tap, but not enough godly wisdom. James writes, "If one of you is wise and understanding, let him show this in practice through a humility filled with good sense. Should you instead nurse bitter jealousy and selfish ambition in your hearts, at least refrain from arrogant and false claims against the truth. Wisdom like this does not come from above. It is earthbound, a kind of animal, even devilish, and cunning. Where there is jealousy and strife, there also are inconstancy and all kinds of vile behavior. Wisdom from above, by contrast, is first of all innocent. It is also peaceable, lenient, docile, rich in sympathy and the kindly deeds that are its fruits, impartial and sincere" (Jas 3:13-17).

Environments which will produce this kind of harvest in us are from God; the others should be carefully discerned. A healthy balance of groups and relationships which foster God's wisdom can greatly help to form us in wisdom and grace.

Natural Creation

Meditation on the natural creation is the third means of developing the Christian mind. The beauty and harmony of God's handiwork bring us into a deeper awareness of who God is and how we can know him. A basic understanding of the redeeming gift of God shows us that "grace builds on the natural." Even primitive man experienced God in nature. He sensed in creation a power beyond himself—a power that was responsible for human life, mountains, trees, water, and the myriad of created things, a power that was to be worshipped. God's revelation of himself has always built on this understanding. As man's awareness became more developed, the personal nature of God became clearer. The fullness of this process is the enfleshment of God in Jesus. Jesus taught man to see God as "Abba," the natural Jewish father. His teachings about the Kingdom of God were contained in stories of normal events and created things.

As we contemplate the natural creation, we deepen our understanding of life and God's ways. This type of understanding is more a matter of perception than intellectual knowledge. We must learn how to see the natural ways of God. As we dwell on the created, we come to know the Creator in a more intimate way.

This ability to be at one with nature is not easy for men in a computerized, industrial age. We are surrounded with technology that obscures the power and beauty of nature, often even denying the very authority of God. It takes work to get behind this technological complexity and penetrate the mystery of nature.

Through grace, I am beginning to sense colors, odors, textures, patterns in nature that I never have seen before. Planting a garden and watching seeds actually grow, I can better understand the parables of Jesus. The spectacle of an ocean surf, operating without a manmade energy source, stirs my mind;

the life-giving flow of a stream brings me into deeper union with God. The miracles of human birth, life, and death fit into a pattern of beauty and mystery.

The Spirit wants to teach today's man about the simple beauty of life. We can learn and transform parts of our mind by allowing him the time to do it. This doesn't mean chucking our jobs, homes, and gadgets, but simply allowing ourselves the freedom to move around those things to receive the gift of life in nature. As the priest-poet Gerard Manley Hopkins wrote, "The world is charged with the grandeur of God."

Study has a broad sense when used in formation of the mind. It includes reading, media, electronic devices, teaching resources, environments, and all the tools available for us to cooperate with the Holy Spirit in our intellectual renewal and formation.

Ways to Study

Reading

For many of us, reading is the best way to study. This is also the means which is most suited to retaining what we study. The human mind initially retains over 85 percent of what is perceived visually; therefore, lasting knowledge usually comes to us from the printed word and other visual sources. Long-term retention is best when we can apply what we learn to our current concerns.

The most important source for daily study should be the scriptures. A father should regularly study the Bible—not just during prayer time or when he reads liturgical selections to his family. He needs a time when he can dig into the sacred books and uncover the historical background and social implications of what is written. There are many ways to study scripture. At its simplest, study should involve a portion of scripture with a good commentary to explain it. The commentary provides background about the passage and insight into its meaning. This type of daily study should move slowly through one book of the Bible at a time. This is different from using the scriptures during prayer, when we should allow our use of the Bible to be led by the Spirit in the context of our daily time with the Lord.

The best time for my scripture study seems to be in the late evening. Just before falling asleep, I usually take ten to fifteen minutes to review a passage of scripture and its commentary. I tend to sleep better when the last thoughts of the day are focused on the Lord.

In addition to daily scripture study, we should read and learn from spiritual and secular books. With inexpensive paperback editions, everyone can afford to purchase good books, borrow them from friends, or frequent a local library. I do not have the space here to give detailed advice about a reading program. The only word I'd like to give in this regard is a warning to be sure that you are reading at least as much of God's word as man's. Pick carefully from among the many available spiritual books. Use common sense and try to concentrate on one book at a time. Ask the Spirit to direct you toward material you can use *now*. Your reading should be addressed to the needs in your life; the purpose of reading is not just to increase your pool of information.

In addition to books, there should be a controlled flow of good Christian periodicals into your home. Treat magazines like books. Subscribe only to what you can read! In our home we try to keep it down to a few spiritual magazines for the teens and adults and at least one for the younger children. Today there is no problem in getting a wide selection of magazines for the entire family.

Media

John J. Delaney, a retired editor of Catholic books, recently commented, "The glamor of the electronic media tends to put into the shade what those of us in the book field consider the greatest means of communication ever devised—the book. TV only has a momentary impact and newspapers make a daily impact, but books written centuries ago are still available and still have an enormous influence in this last quarter of the twentieth century."

While the impact of media is short-lived, its influence on our minds is overwhelming. According to a *U.S. News and World Report* survey of institutions which most influence American society: television, radio, and newspapers consistently outrank the family and organized religion. For most men today, opinions and values are strongly influenced, if not molded, by TV and daily papers.

We must learn how to control and limit the negative effects of TV and journalism in our homes. A steady diet of bad news and secular opinion distorts our minds and competes strongly with the Good News which we are commissioned to be. I dropped daily newspapers and TV news from our home several years ago. I can honestly say that we haven't missed anything important. We have also avoided much of the frustration and confusion which the "global village" provides. There are some excellent programs on TV, but we are very selective about what we watch.

The principle operating here is that a Christian home should be a place where the power of God has won a visible victory over the world. This victory includes our ability to personally regulate the media, not expecting others to do it for us. We can use the media for our study, but it requires personal discipline and good discernment. Search out good programming which will build your faith. Avoid the rest. "The reign of God is also like a dragnet thrown into the lake, which collected all sorts of things. When it was full they hauled it ashore and sat down to put what was worthwhile into containers. What was useless they threw away" (Mt 13:47-48).

Tapes

Bob Mumford, a noted Christian speaker, has said that the Kingdom of God runs on C-90 cassettes. Perhaps this is an exaggeration, but one of the best tools we have for study is taped teaching on the Christian life. We can listen to tapes alone, in groups, and especially when we are performing repetitive manual tasks. I like to listen to tapes while driving alone on extended trips. Although we retain less of what we hear than what we see, the higher volume of material which can be covered in tapes makes up for it. Tapes are fairly inexpensive and easily reproduced. Although nothing can replace a living speaker, tapes can provide something of the impact of a human teacher.

Sharing Groups

When individuals with common values come together in a group to share their ideas and experiences, a multiplying effect occurs. This is called "synergism." The group takes on a life of its own. "Refrain not from speaking at the proper time, and hide not away your wisdom; for it is through speech that wisdom becomes known" (Sir 4:23-24). Everyone grows in a group where the members share their wisdom and gain insight from others.

The key to effective study in a group is the degree of common values held by the members and the quality of direction provided. Getting into a specialized group is not too difficult since most churches and renewal movements provide such opportunities. However, leaving a group is not as easy as joining one. Sharing groups are effective when relationships are close and healthy; they do not succeed only because of ideas which are shared. Therefore when you join a group, you should expect to get involved with the lives of the other people.

Sharing groups should not become counseling sessions where the most articulate people dominate and "minister" to the needy. For the group to succeed, everyone must see himself as someone who needs the others. Small groups should provide support and affirmation for each member.

I would strongly encourage every Christian father to become a part of a regular sharing group with other men who want to deepen in their vocation as a husband and father. Participation in such a group should be a regular part of your study program. It should be a place where men can study each other as models of grace, saying with Paul, "Be imitators of me, my brothers. Take as your guide those who follow the example we set" (Phil 3:17).

Many groups form around the scriptures. These usually fall into two categories: scripture sharing and Bible study.

The scripture sharing group comes together to read and prayerfully reflect on the personal implications of a scripture passage. I've experienced this type of group at the House of Prayer Experience (H.O.P.E.)—a Christian renewal center based in Convent Station, New Jersey. There, some people gather every day to prayerfully review a passage of scripture, usually one chapter, then share what that passage means to each person. These groups do not attempt to use commentaries and they avoid difficult theology. Rather, they exist for personal reflection on God's word today. Scripture sharing could be especially well suited for married couples, to extend their normal dialogue.

By contrast, the Bible study group attempts serious study, utilizing commentaries and other tools. A good friend of mine, Pete Radice, has been a part of a Bible study for several years, and has grown in knowledge of God's word as a result. It is a possible model for other such groups. The group is made up of men and women who work together for a large chemical firm. They meet once a week in a company conference room during the lunch hour. The group is ecumenical and encourages a wide expression of scriptural understanding. A different person leads and moderates each week. The focus of the session is to penetrate the meaning of a passage. Everyone has a chance to give an interpretation of the passage based on his understanding of it, gained through study. Many Bible study groups already operate at places of employment, and most firms would encourage them. Such groups stress building relationships among the members as well as deepening everyone's knowledge of God's word.

Seminars and Conferences

The latest trend for intense Christian study seems to be the seminar or large conference. This tool for study, now being used extensively in secular industry, brings teachers and learners together for a concentrated session. It removes people from their ordinary environments and can effectively cover a large body of material. The main disadvantages of seminars are the cost and the tendency for people who attend to become exhausted. However, used carefully, the conference setting can expand our vision and provide good teaching in specific areas.

The same caution against overindulgence applies to conferences as to reading. Conferences are artificial situations which can become irrelevant to our everyday life. We should attend these sessions with a desire to apply what we learn, not to just acquire valuable but unusable knowledge, or worse, to escape from our real lives. Seminars and conferences should propel us into our daily environment.

Retreats

While most forms of study are active, the spiritual retreat is a more passive way to learn. As a pleasant change to the pace of modern life, the retreat is a time for relaxation and refreshment. The study we experience comes from within, as God sorts out our lives. During a retreat, we discover our inner self and meditate on the wonder of God who dwells there. A regular retreat is essential to a Christian father. It is a time for him to come to the Lord and be refreshed in body, mind, and spirit.

While most people take retreats at centers which offer liturgy and inspirational talks, the Lord may occasionally want us to retreat to a private place where we can simply listen to him. This kind of "desert" retreat is best suited for those times when major decisions are pending. After we have sorted out all the human wisdom, we should go to God in stillness and listen only to him. I try not to make any major decisions until I have had this kind of period to allow the Spirit to shape my mind.

Study Patterns

The study program for Christian fathers which has been outlined here will work within our normal daily patterns. We do not have to withdraw from life in order to learn. Our education is meant to be more of the "co-op" or practical variety. The needs of our family point us toward the required wisdom, and we promptly apply what we learn.

When we fail to take a practical view of study as something to be integrated into our normal routine, we run the risk of becoming frustrated. Trying to do too much too quickly, we can get overwhelmed and do nothing. We should look for little changes in our patterns which can open our minds to the Holy Spirit. Since study is our mental food, the rules for good eating and digestion can roughly apply. Sudden changes in our patterns will cause indigestion; gradual changes can make a lasting difference.

The changes we should make require decision and follow-through. We have to *decide* to read the Bible or to get away for a retreat. Then we must *act* on our decision. The changes we make today will look small a few years from now, but any beginning is better than none at all. Take the most pressing need first. For most men, this is daily Bible study. It is the best place to begin. Without a growing scriptural base for our fatherhood, we cannot proceed very far.

When considering changes in your study patterns, use some of these principles drawn from nature:

> Growth occurs seasonally through epochs and periods. Try to blend change and growth with the seasons of your life. What is natural for you now?

> Vines will eventually kill a healthy tree. Cut your ties to environments which have not yielded any fruit after a reasonable waiting period.

> Water your seeds regularly. The grace of continual prayer and a healthy sacramental feeding will cause the seeds of wisdom to grow faster.

One of the biggest hurdles which most men must overcome in pursuing a program of study is mental laziness. We are quickly becoming a media-formed, spectator-oriented society. We are inclined to passivity. Fathers must fight this tendency and aggressively seek the wisdom they need for a particular season of their lives. A "laissez-faire" attitude is not sufficient to motivate an already busy man to make the necessary decisions and to follow through on them.

My own mental laziness was caused by never having cultivated good study habits as a young man. My school years did not challenge me, so I was never motivated to stretch my mind and increase my capacity. This can be an even bigger problem for our children who seem to have fewer standards in school, less homework, and more formation from the media. We should set a good example in our families and encourage reading, discussion, and writing to stimulate the wonderful mental faculties which God has provided.

The Lord eventually transformed my mental laziness into a hunger for spiritual knowledge, a true need. The Holy Spirit, invited by my prayer, stirred this hunger into a quest to know God, and he also directed me to the right sources for study. Look at your deepest needs as a man, as a husband and a father. These needs will provide the direction for your study.

Some personal examples of how my study habits have changed may be helpful to other fathers. These are changes which I've been led to make. They are not meant to be hard and fast rules. Seek the Lord for his plan in your particular situation.

A few years ago I was spending much time in my company car, traveling on business. I had insisted that my car have an FM radio so I could listen to good music, but as all-day news programs became more popular, I turned increasingly to them. The depth of my addiction to media news became evident during the Watergate crisis. I was so engrossed in the dirt which was surfacing that I found myself delaying business meetings to stay in my car and listen to the latest news.

I was finally convinced of my problem while discussing it with a group of close friends. They admitted that the bizarre details of this national tragedy were causing them the same kind of mental distraction. After praying about it, I made a commitment not to use my car radio during Lent. The grace of that holy season and the support of my friends motivated the beginning of a new pattern.

The first few days were tough, but in time it was clear that this decision was in God's plan. Instead of the radio I listened to taped teachings or just enjoyed the silence. Eventually this change became permanent; my travel time is now committed to spiritual growth through Christian study.

This change led me to an understanding of how media news, if not taken in measured portions, forms our minds and distorts the Good News. I saw how my wife and children were absorbed by the latest sports, fashions, and advertising. These are not bad things in themselves, but God showed me that we were abusing them. After praying and discussing it with Anna, I took another step and cancelled our daily paper. This was difficult at first but as we saw the positive effects on the entire family, we were encouraged to curb other areas, like TV. These changes have freed our minds for the Lord and our time for each other. Today we talk together more, read more, and are even able to have some quiet time. The cost of these benefits has been to miss a few "crises," many of which were only exaggerated by the media to drum up interest in the news.

Changes in our established patterns of behavior will not endure unless we share them with others and invite *accountability* into our lives. The American image of the "rugged individualist" creates great westerns, but it doesn't provide the help a man of God needs to live the Gospel.

Accountability bolsters our self-discipline and uncovers hidden fears. It is a protection against our weaknesses. Accountability in our personal life must be freely offered to someone who loves and knows us. This can be an individual or a group—possibly the sharing group you may be part of. Choose the person or persons carefully. If you are surrounded with people who have the same weaknesses as you have and who do not want to change, you may have to find new friends, or entirely new surroundings to find the growth which God wants for you.

Our study should lead to transformation of our personal and corporate lives. To be effective, it must be predicated on a personal decision to *become* what we have learned we should be. That circumcision of the heart is only possible when the knowledge we take in is directed by the Holy Spirit. The Father sends the Spirit to teach us and form our minds on a "need to know" basis. This works with the natural hunger placed in us at Baptism: the need to know Jesus. This is the goal.

Jesus is the focal point of all Christian study because: (1) he alone reveals the Father. "No one knows the Son except the Father and no one knows the Father except the Son—and anyone to whom the Son wishes to reveal him" (Lk 10:22); and (2) he interprets the mysteries of God. "When the disciples got near him, they asked him, 'Why do you speak to them in parables?' He answered: 'To you has been given a knowledge of the mysteries of the reign of God, but it has not been given to the others'" (Mt 13:10-11).

Part Three

Personal Maturity in Christ

CHAPTER SEVEN

Balance:
Fullness and Order

The first of three keys to personal maturity in Christ is balance. The other two are simplicity and fidelity to covenant. The importance of these three characteristics—balance, simplicity, and fidelity to covenant—were made clear to me during a difficult time. I learned about them while reaching out to serve a close friend whose wife had just died in a tragic automobile accident. In a crisis, we are confronted with the weakness and the temporary nature of our human condition. At such times a man turns to God for strength and that's what my friend and I did. A few weeks after the accident, Tom and I, along with some close friends, took a short retreat at a secluded Carmelite monastery in the mountains of upper New York State.

Anna and I met Tom and his wife Judy through our involvement in the Cursillo Movement. Our relationship had a uniqueness to it. The wonderful chemistry of Christian friendship is so different than the superficiality we sometimes experience elsewhere in life. Tom and Judy were special friends. We had celebrated a fullness in Jesus together and our families had grown close in the few months we shared. The news of Judy's sudden death shot through me like a bolt of lightning. What seemed so good was now gone. I asked God for an answer which could make some sense out of this tragedy. Why, Lord? Why a young wife and mother with a wonderful marriage and two beautiful children? Why Lord? Why Judy?

As Tom and I spent time walking in the woods together, the

loving presence of Jesus brought about a deeper peace than either of us had felt before. The peace of Christ slowly erased our need for answers. Just as the death of my father had awakened a new sense of my fatherhood, this crisis now opened me to listen to God more deeply. When we're available to him, God usually takes the opportunity to speak. His word came to me in quiet prayer and loving sharing between brothers. He revealed the importance of balance, simplicity, and fidelity to covenant.

I didn't understand what those words meant at that time, but the Lord has since shown me how they were to be three essential characteristics of my growth in the Lord and especially of my Christian fatherhood. God's word to me on that retreat didn't come from a burning bush, but when the Spirit speaks to your heart, you know it. I had heard the Lord, but didn't fully grasp what he meant or what I was supposed to do.

The word I had received was meant to prepare me for a more complete revelation which would come a few years later through a deeper release of God's power: baptism in the Holy Spirit. With the Spirit's direction, my understanding increased. The next four chapters will deal with the keys to personal maturity in more detail, but let's begin with balance and what it means for a Christian father.

Jesus calls a father to a radical stance. He is to live a whole and holy life, not only for himself, but as a sign to his family and the world. God wants men who will become signs of faith, hope, and love—contradictions to the often confusing pace of modern life. He wants men who can take what is good and holy in this world and use it for the Kingdom of God.

God's Balance

Sometimes it's easier to explain spiritual things through analogies than through abstract concepts. As I searched for a good example to describe the process of coming into God's balance, the image of a surfer seemed to convey the dynamic which needs to be understood.

A surfer must do two things to keep his balance and ride the big waves. As he gets in front of a wave, he must be at the right point on his board, and his body must be in position to counter-balance the forces set up by the surf and the wind. He is a man who is dealing with a moving situation; only the right combination of leverage and body stance keeps him on top of that situation. Since forces outside his control are shifting around him, he must be constantly alert to accurately adjust his position to counter-balance them. He doesn't simply find a safe spot on the board and stay there. He must be fearless; ready and willing to move with the surf and wind. As he becomes proficient, the surfer begins to relax and enjoy the challenge. An accomplished surfer can look up, not down at his feet. He has acquired the technique he needs to keep his balance.

A father who is seeking God's balance in his life must also be on top of the often turbulent circumstances of the world around him. He is striving to reach that point where he can enjoy the family which God has given him, not just stand up and survive. He is developing that unique stance which will allow him to live in the world and radiate the peace of Christ. Like the surfer, he must be alert and constantly ready to adjust his position in order to stay on the leading edge of the waves of life. Although the surf and the wind are trying to push him under, he knows how to resist them, and even use them to stay upright. He is a man who is mastering the art of balance. As he captures the fundamentals of fatherhood, he can take his attention off himself and look ahead.

The gift of balance comes through our relationship with the Father. Jesus leads us to the point of God's balance. He has been sent to show us how to stay on top of every circumstance of life.

The sign of balance is peace. The Christian father must search for the stance in life, at any particular time, which produces this sense in his heart. The peace of Christ comes, not because we're free of problems, but because we've allowed ourselves to be led to the posture and position which God has selected for us at this moment in our lives.

The great teacher and giver of peace is Jesus. He is at the balance point, offering peace as his first greeting to his disciples. He walked on the water and he wants to teach us how to do it too. When the first disciples were terrified in the midst of storms (Mt 8:23-27 and 14:22-33), the presence and the authority of Jesus calmed them and brought them peace.

The Christian father seeking God's balance must look to the example of Jesus, who walked peacefully through human and spiritual circumstances which would have driven the strongest of men into a panic. Jesus faced conflict, disappointment, hatred, death and the worst pain of all—total rejection. He was able to do this for one reason: He was continually in an intimate relationship with his Father. He kept his balance because the Father never left him alone.

The situations we face as fathers are different only in degree from those Jesus encountered. We too face troubles, and we too are drawn into panic and fear. Jesus showed us how to master that fear. Balance comes by staying in close relationship with the Father, and by following the leading of the Spirit to the point where we experience the peace of Christ.

What Is the Balanced Life?

A balanced life is a rich, full, and productive one. Being of Italian heritage, I appreciated a recent TV commercial which showed a robust woman trying to explain how special her pizza was. She struggled with some English words, then threw her hands up and said, "You know, *abbondanza!*" The Italian word is expressive; it means "abundance." God wants *abbondanza* for us. The quality of the abundant life he wants for fathers often goes beyond our ability to express it with familiar words. Our limited expectations tend to limit what God can do. It is therefore important to raise our expectations, and to understand more fully the abundance God has for us. These are some qualities of a balanced father's life.

A balanced life is a full life. I've felt some sense of abundance when I'm able to be strong and effective at the end of a busy day. The opposite feeling comes when I've struggled all day and can't seem to accomplish anything. On the days when my effort, not God's will, pushes me in frustrating circles, I feel exhausted at night. The abundant life which God promises will fill our days with productive activity. When the day is spent, we will be happy, not wrung out. To be productive, we allow God to lead us; we do not try to lead ourselves. Expect more. Jesus' words are clear. "The thief comes only to steal and slaughter and destroy. I came that they might have life and have it to the full" (Jn 10:10).

A balanced life is a holy life. Jesus didn't just speak about the Kingdom in nice words; he showed us the way to live. Above all, Jesus was holy. Our false images of holiness tend to distort his gospel and prevent us from experiencing the fullness God wants for us. We envision "holy men" as little plastic saints with sad faces and restricted lives. Jesus wasn't that kind of a man and he didn't call men like that to be his disciples. He walked boldly into life and drew genuine holiness out of men who were living normal lives. He showed us the balance between God's life and man's humanity. In Jesus, holiness and wholeness were one.

A sign in the gospels of the wholeness of Jesus is the picture of little children flocking around him. Any father knows how quickly a child can spot a phony. Children have an uncanny ability to point to the truth. They won't believe a man's words unless they accurately reflect how he lives. Jesus' authority was based on his integrity. His words and his actions were one. God wants this kind of spirituality for all fathers—a holiness which produces wholeness in those who surround them. The Church doesn't need more preaching or more theology; it needs men who are speaking and acting like Jesus.

A balanced life is a real life. Fathers who strive to become holy men of God can fall into a common trap. We can speak so negatively about "the world" and our "flesh" that we shun them and try to live in a totally spiritual realm. We forget that Jesus came into history to redeem our humanity, not to condemn or destroy it. The Son of Man came into our world to bring it the fullness of the life of the Father. Creation has become distorted and sinful, but God has not given up on it and

neither can we. Living in Christ, we bring that life to the poor
and hungry who have never heard of it or seen anyone live it.

I learned something about the task of living a balanced but
real life by learning how to handle the unexpected. As a successful salesman, I learned how valuable my time was. I scheduled it carefully, trying to fill my days with meetings and
lunches which would produce profitable sales. However, when
dealing with top executives, I had to expect last-minute
changes in their schedules. I would be all set for a round of
important meetings when someone's secretary would call and
cancel out because of an emergency.

In responding to situations like these, I had to give my frustration to the Lord, stop grumbling, and ask Jesus: "Now what
do you want me to do with this gift of free time?" My life as a
husband and father is full of such shifts and changes. Until I
learned to embrace them as gifts, it was hard to see a situation
from God's perspective. We need God's grace, and the direction of the Holy Spirit to bring us to the point of balance in
every situation.

A balanced life is a life of harmony. The balance that we seek as
fathers is a life where things work together. Quite often, it is
the surprises of the Spirit which cultivate, enrich, and balance
our lives. The Spirit's work creates harmony from all the dis-
parate elements of our lives. Our human spirit strives for perfection and the satisfaction of our will. God's Spirit, at work in
us, glorifies the Father and his will.

I started to understand the harmony God wanted me to experience in my busy life while attending concerts by the
Philadelphia Orchestra. The ability of a fine conductor like Eu-
gene Ormandy to blend numerous individual performers and
sounds into a harmonic whole gave me some appreciation for
the action of God's Spirit in us. The first time we attended a
concert, I was amazed at the seemingly confused situation on
stage before the conductor arrived. Each musician was tuning
up and playing his instrument as he pleased. Their individual
gifts and the quality of the instruments were lost in a mass of
confusion. However, when the concert began, they blended
into a unified sound. There were expensive instruments and

talented individuals, but it took a gifted conductor, and a yield-ing to his lead, to bring out fine music.

There is no music for us without the harmony which the Spirit brings. Our lives resemble the confusion of the tune-up period, until the Spirit steps onto our stage and calls us into balance and harmony. That kind of harmony begins as we move with God and play the part which he has planned for us. "God is a God, not of confusion, but of peace" (1 Cor 14:33).

A Livable Pace

To get a clear understanding of how we lose our balance, let's look at the pace of our lives. Do we rush from meeting to meeting, from one activity to another? Do we tend to grade the people around us as "important" and "unimportant"? Do we try to spend more time with "important" people and cut short our time with others? Do we allow enough room in our lives for the unplanned people and events, the surprises of the Spirit? Do we enjoy life or do we simply accept survival? Is there an answer to the merry-go-round many fathers find themselves on? I believe there is. We can lead the full lives God has called us to, but it means a new pace. A livable one!

To realize the balance which the Lord promises, most fathers will have to make some difficult decisions and changes. The first is to resist the pressure to constantly "do more." This pressure is fierce and it comes from many sources, both from the secular world and from the Church. Many fathers are con-stantly busy because they want to serve real needs, but often the deeper motivation for busyness is guilt.

We feel guilty from trying to be all things to all people. The ideals of our modern world increasingly call for more: more education, more money, more exercise, more friends, more, more, more. All this activity is supposed to produce self-fulfillment. Instead, it yields exhaustion and frustration. The only thing most of us need more of is Jesus and his peace in our hearts. The love of Christ is available to us when we turn to him for it. It is not based on what we do. We do not earn the abundant life by doing more; it is pure gift. We learn how to receive that gift by resisting the pressure to conform and constantly do more.

The new tempo that God wants of us is not a static thing. Our pace will change, depending on the grace and the need of any particular moment. Some circumstances will call for a slow stroll; others, a medium jog; some may require a full sprint. As we discover the right pace for each situation, we get into step with the Shepherd.

Some time ago, my frantic pace of life brought me to an important spiritual insight. The Lord showed me that I needed to breathe in an entirely new way—both physically and spiritually.

This awareness dawned one day when I had just collapsed in a chair after trying to do too many things at once. Although I was exhausted, I hadn't accomplished much. Breathing very heavily, I was taking in oxygen at the wrong pace; gulping air, not drawing it in evenly. After recovering my normal rate of breathing, I sensed the Lord showing me how this physical experience illustrated a spiritual principle.

When we are out of shape physically, we can sustain a high level of activity only with difficulty. We have to gulp oxygen rapidly, and soon we must quit. However, when physically fit, we can keep going for a long time. We might breathe heavily at the beginning of exercise, but soon our breathing settles into a regular, shallow rhythm. The body is working hard, but it can take in and use life-giving oxygen very efficiently. For the most part, that's what being fit means. The key to this kind of physical fitness is training the body to breathe properly, and finding a pace of work or exercise that doesn't overtax our heart and lungs.

The same is true of spiritual fitness. When we are not in step with Jesus, we quickly run down after exerting ourselves. We can keep going for a little while, but soon we lie down, spiritually exhausted. But if we train ourselves and find God's pace, we can breathe much more efficiently. Sitting exhausted in my chair that day, I realized that part of God's balance for a father was learning to breathe spiritually in a new way.

About this time I heard Fr. George Maloney speak about

Christian meditation. Using Fr. Maloney's insights, I established a new pattern of spiritual breathing. I learned to breathe in the Word "Jesus" and to breathe out the Father's nature, "Abba." As I allowed Jesus to be drawn into my life in steady ways, the reflection of God which I gave to my family became clearer. We become stronger Christian fathers as this process takes hold. As our intake of fresh spiritual insight and experience becomes a normal part of our lives, we will grow in our balance. The days must end when a big gulp of Jesus once a week satisfies us. In responding to our fatherhood, we cannot be a holy man only when it's convenient. Our loved ones need a reflection of God that is constant and strong.

Emotional Balance

God's call for fathers also involves a balance between the masculine and feminine side of our natures. Usually, this means that the feminine side of our personhood needs development. This is the part of us which deals with emotions, feelings, and sensitivity. It can be a startling experience for a man to face the softness which God wants to create on this side of his personality. This is an area which is growing in me, but I know that it is important for strong fatherhood.

God created man male and female. The two sexes are complementary. They compose God's image of himself to us. The fall of Adam and Eve caused a part of that image in each of us to die. When man and woman sinned, fragmentation entered their relationship. What God created as complementary and whole, man's rebellion turned into competition and division. Part of this division was a separation between the masculine and feminine dimension of our personalities.

As the Spirit works to bring us into a greater unity with God and those around us, he also restores a unity within us by developing our feminine side. Men need an emotional fullness which includes the softness which we call "feminine." The idea of the "macho" man is distorted. God wants us to capture a vision of wholeness which is an accurate reflection of his creation.

Jesus was the perfect reflection of this balance. He was the model of a fully human and fully alive man. His life shows the complete range of emotions and an unguarded openness to broken people of both sexes. Jesus was a strong man, yet tender as well. His tenderness allowed him to strengthen others, not to defeat them. His strength allowed him to stand up to the authorities and the power brokers of his time. He responded to individual needs, rejecting no one except Satan himself.

Jesus was single-minded about his mission to the Jewish people, yet he was flexible enough to stop and spend some time with a Samaritan woman. Such an ability to switch plans and respond to someone in need is a key element in the emotional fullness fathers need. We face many unplanned circumstances each day and have to handle them without being thrown off balance. Flexibility is a principal characteristic of a whole and holy man.

Jesus is calling fathers into the emotional balance and fullness which he experienced. The seeming opposites of strength and tenderness; determination and flexibility; masculine and feminine are all brought into a creative equilibrium under the Lordship of Jesus. We are his disciples; he sets the pace. Jesus walks before his followers and simply says, "Come follow me." In the same way, a man leads his family. He can say to them, "Come follow me" or as Paul said: "Imitate me." His family wants to hear, "You can trust in our direction, because I'm following Jesus."

Creative Order

The change in my life which I resisted most fiercely had to do with order. I rebelled at the idea; it recalled old images of dry and lifeless routines. I thought order was the opposite of the fullness which Jesus promised. An ordered life had to be a dull life.

I have since learned that order allows both fullness and creativity. In fact, balance in the Christian life is impossible without order. A creative and full fatherhood depends on it as well.

All of creation displays this facet of balance: fullness within the confines of regularity. Consider the seasons of the year. We experience the full range of colors, temperatures and precipitation, yet in the right place and at the proper time. Nature is properly ordered so that its fullness may be released. God wants our lives arranged the same way.

The task of restoring personal order usually begins with our thinking process. Many men tend to carry a whole pile of disordered clutter around in their heads—yesterday's work, the bills that need to be paid, sexual fantasies, worries about problems which haven't happened yet. Much of this is pointless trivia; our minds get bogged down with things which are in the past or which are out of our control. Jesus tells us, "Don't be anxious," yet our mental clutter causes anxiety.

Much of what makes a man anxious stems from a crisis-oriented thinking process. We expect crises and therefore we create them. We deal with problems as if they were all crises, and then we worry about what's ahead. Unfortunately, we become self-fulfilling prophets. Most crises can be avoided by using our minds correctly. We should not dwell on past problems, but instead scan the future for possible problems so we can meet them routinely. In the military we called this "contingency planning." Military staffs have made crisis avoidance into a highly developed science. The staff looks realistically at problems and plans accordingly to meet each one in an ordinary way.

Crisis avoidance planning should only take a small part of our mental energy, but it can remove a lot of anxiety. Eventually these excursions into contingency planning should become almost an unnoticed natural pattern, like the braking and steering we do while driving a car.

If we do not plan for contingencies, we are open to confusion when crises suddenly come. Some crises are productive, but most can and should be avoided. The task of maintaining a home illustrates the point. To avoid problems, we must regularly paint, clear drains, clean, replace worn gaskets, fix faucets, and so on. We could ignore these jobs and hope that things will take care of themselves. But we know that the price of neglect will be a bad leak or a clogged drain. It is far better to organize the wonderful cerebral capacity God has given to us and let crisis become the exception in our lives, not the rule.

Many men will achieve creative order in their lives as they bring their emotions under control. This means learning to face problems objectively, and not be deterred by the normal inconveniences and frustrations which are part of any man's life. When God's order is present, we aren't led any longer by our feelings.

This was a particular problem for me. I had fallen into a pattern of being controlled by the negative emotions of frustration and anger. I was comfortable with this; I even justified it. I felt that a man who had to control his emotions at work all day should have the right to explode and vent those feelings at home. The redeeming power of the Holy Spirit is working overtime in my life to break that old pattern. It is one of the old ways of thinking and acting that is changing.

I'm very conscious of the damage which the imbalance in my emotional order has caused because similar patterns occasionally come out in our home. After watching me explode in uncontrolled anger, it's easy for children to conclude that Dad's way must be okay. As a remedy, I'm struggling to substitute praise and repentance where once anger and resentment controlled me. However, these negative emotions are still strong tendencies, and I do everything possible to avoid being put in a situation where they will erupt. I try to foresee frustration and steer around it. This defensive tactic is my part in the process of emotional healing; the rest is up to the Lord. He is working on the root hurts in my heart which caused the problem in the first place. As this negative pattern in me is changing, the problem it has caused in my home is also fading. Today, we don't tolerate uncontrolled anger. We call it what it is—sin. When it happens, we repent immediately and go on. This allows us to approach situations according to objective norms, not according to our feelings.

A word of caution: As fathers reach the point of God's balance in their lives, they should beware of making order an end in itself. Order becomes an impediment when it is pursued for its own sake. I learned this lesson when I found that my natural gift for planning was causing a problem. My ability to plan worked very well in business. It allowed me to solve complex business problems and to accomplish difficult tasks. I could lay out a critical path of events, plan systems, and organize schedules.

This is a good gift, but it became an idol. In planning my time and my appointments tightly, my mind was constantly seeking ever-greater efficiency. Attempting to get an early start, I hardly ever saw my family in the morning. I managed my afternoons so as to take advantage of the last possible opportunity in the day to see a client. When I arrived home, it was often too late to have dinner with my family. I certainly used my gift of planning, but for which kingdom?

I gradually became aware that I was making scheduling into an idol. As I sought the Lord's will for my life, he taught me about creative order. I learned how to use my gift to love and serve. God's order creates enough discipline and structure in our lives so that we are free to *love* more, not to just *do* more.

Creative order comes from the Spirit and leads us to balance. We are taught how to do a number of important things, in their proper sequence, without exhausting our minds or bodies. The image of the Holy Spirit as a dove can emphasize this truth. The dove must be held very gently. If we squeeze too tightly, we will crush her; if we hold her too loosely, she will fly away. This is the way order should operate in our lives: a firm presence, but gently applied so that we are able to love more freely.

Signs of Balance

When God is in control of a man's life, his presence is evident in some very definite signs. The action of the Spirit is not invisible. It produces changes which we can see and feel. Jesus promised that his followers would experience evident changes, ones that would give life to those who saw them.

The key sign of a balanced life in God's creative order is *openness* to other people. A peaceful man seems to invite others to come into his life. He is willing to listen to others, especially his wife and children. Because God has balanced his life, he responds rather than reacts. His response is genuine concern about others; it isn't spiritual rhetoric, which side-steps the other person's real need. The peaceful man takes time to listen. He is blessed with a listening heart which is open, available, and vulnerable to others. To listen with one's heart means to listen "between the lines." A man of balance is at peace with himself; he hears what someone wants to say, but cannot.

The balanced man is also known by his ability to deal effectively with *emotional pressure*. He isn't controlled by anger and hostility which are so much a part of the "old man." When a father replaces an angry reaction with a gentle response, a new sense of God's presence begins to fill his home.

Another sign of a balanced life is the hunger for increased *personal discipline*. This discipline changes our schedules and plans into tools for loving others. Discipline makes our minds alert. We are not caught off balance by the normal problems of life. We are able to deal with crises. The balanced man does all he can and doesn't expect God to cover up for his laziness. But he does no more than his best, expecting God to work in his life and in the lives of those around him.

For myself, the most evident sign of new balance is the *ability to adapt* to unexpected change. I am learning to expect change; I even welcome it. I don't fight it any longer. Where schedules were once my idol and a bondage, I now use them to create more room for the Spirit to work.

These are some of the signs of a balanced life. The wholeness of God's creation is fully alive in the man of balance and a hunger for holiness is his driving force. He is an accurate reflection of God. He has grasped the forces of life, and by way of grace is bringing them into creative order.

CHAPTER EIGHT

How To Invest Your Time

A few years ago, my children gave me a banner for Christmas. The title was "Take Time" and it offered the following suggestions:

Take Time to think
It is the source of power

Take Time to play
It is the secret of perpetual youth

Take Time to read
It is the foundation of wisdom

Take Time to pray
It is the greatest power on earth

Take Time to love and be loved
It is a God-given privilege

Take Time to be friendly
It is the road to happiness

Take Time to laugh
It is the music of the soul

Take Time to give
It is too short a day to be selfish.

When I received that banner, my life was far from God's balance. I hung it on the wall facing my desk at the office. During especially hectic times I'd look up and read those words over again. The message my children gave me finally hit home: Their Dad was too busy to do what the banner suggested. God was speaking to me in his loving, gentle way. As I heard him and began looking at how I used time, a desire for a new pace of life grew in me.

An honest look at how I spent my time revealed that the busyness which seemed to envelop me was mostly my own creation. I liked it! The appearance of "looking busy" made me feel important. I could control my pace, yet I had chosen an unnecessarily busy one. This is a very common approach taken by businessmen, especially salesmen. A successful man is supposed to be very busy, so those who want to be successful manage to look that way.

God is calling us to holiness and wholeness, not busyness. He wants to change how we spend our days. Time is a gift from God; it is a resource which we can invest where we choose. It is also one resource which we have in abundance. All of us have the free gift of twenty-four hours each day. We decide where and with whom to invest those hours.

When we are asked for an accounting of the time which has been given to us, we should be able to say, "Father, I spent most of it on the Kingdom." Time invested in the Kingdom of God—especially in our families—will yield abundant life.

Jesus is the Lord of Time

Time measures a dimension of this world. Thus, it is part of the creation Jesus came to save. By raising Jesus to glory, the Father has given him dominion over all created things, including time. He can redeem our abuse of this gift, just as he brings redemption to other parts of creation.

Jesus wants a reorientation in our use of time, a renewal which includes both our minds and our behavior. He wants to reach the causes of our weaknesses, not just their effects. This kind of radical change must begin with a stirring of the Holy

Spirit, who creates both the hunger and the answers to our questions.

I never had difficulty with efficient use of time. My problem centered on investing my resource in the wrong kingdom. Two examples of how my use of time changed should illustrate the importance the Lord attaches to this area.

As a salesman for many years, I spent many hours traveling. In early days I traveled mostly by car, but later, as the business became more complex, often by train and plane. Paradoxically, my need to travel on business grew greater as I surrendered my life to the Lord. An inner tension developed in me. On one side was a man of God who knew that his pace was too fast; on the other, was the achiever who wasn't yet willing to make the decisions which were necessary. As the tension mounted, I knew something had to change. It didn't happen overnight but eventually Jesus redeemed my travel time! Within a short while, I decided to use those hours of travel for study and growth in the Spirit.

That simple decision made a drastic change. I began to carry a small New Testament in my brief case, and a good Christian book or magazine with me on the road. A tape recorder in my car allowed me to hear Christian teachings while traveling to and from airports and train stations. It was like discovering a new treasure. I went through the entire New Testament in about six months, just by reading a little each day. Instead of squandering my time, I was able to put it to good use.

The second example relates more directly to my family. We have six children, a dog, many good friends, and relatives. Our home often becomes a gathering place for Christians, and food shopping is a big item on our list of things to do. For years, I had always done a fair share of that shopping, yet I resented it as an infringement on my time. After all, my time was valuable. I felt that the hours spent pushing a shopping cart and hauling bags of groceries were wasted. I was right. They were wasted. This time was wasted because I didn't know what to do with it or how to view it.

One day, after listening to me grumble about all the time shopping took, a Christian friend gently suggested that I consider using that time to be with one of our children. He said, "I always make it a practice to run errands and do things with my children if I can." What a simple idea! I began inviting a child to shop with me. They were surprised and happy to spend some extra time with their father. Today, food shopping has become a blessed opportunity for forming the children, because I've learned how to view that time as a resource for fatherhood.

As Jesus becomes Lord of our time, he will lead in a way which releases us from the bondage to our past. As the grace of the present moment frees us, we can release our guilt, especially that which might weigh heavily on a man who is approaching the Lord, in the autumn or the winter of his life.

We needn't burden our hearts about the years which were wasted serving another master. God wants us looking forward. The Lord of time has a specific plan for each man and each family. The detailed route and the timing of your particular plan is only for God to know, but this much I'm sure of: God's plan is *never* late.

Prime Time

Christian fathers can learn to devote their "prime time" to their most important responsibilities. Prime time is our best time. It is not necessarily the greatest amount of time. Instead, it is the time in our day or week when we are most effective and attentive to the Holy Spirit.

The quality time we invest should be directed to prayer, study, and loving actions—the fundamentals of Christian fatherhood. The first priority is prayer. It is more productive to spend fifteen minutes of prime time praising and glorifying the Father than to spend an hour when one's mind is congested. We should pray at the *best* time of our day. It often takes a certain amount of experimentation and effort to discover when that is.

Study also requires prime time, and usually a sizeable amount of it. Our study should occur when we can concentrate and absorb what God wants to teach us. At one time in my life, the time I spent on business trips was best for my study. For men whose schedules are more predictable, the lunch hour or coffee breaks might be better. You might also want to reconsider how much time you spend on TV, newspapers and other leisure activities. Perhaps you can invest a portion of that time in study.

The third leg of the tripod of fundamentals is loving action— prime time spent with those we are called to love and care for. Being present to a family or an aging parent just can't be done on the run; it requires planning and choices. A father won't spend enough time with those who need him most if he leaves this to chance. Many men think that relationship with their wives and children will just "happen." It rarely will. A man has to plan for it and invest the time needed.

This point may sound self-evident, but few fathers follow it. How many men do you know have a specific time each day just for their wives? How many fathers allocate parts of their day to talk to their children? Effective communication takes time and it has to be prime time. Could you imagine what confusion would develop in a business if the owner saw his top executives only when he had some extra time? What would happen to a manager whose own work was so confused that he couldn't spend time with those whose work he was managing? Most fathers can see that regular communications are needed in the efficient running of any business; shouldn't this same attitude be taken toward our families? We can easily get our priorities reversed and find ourselves concentrating heavily on the need to work, eat, and sleep—things which only support the *real* priorities. Admittedly, our schedules are full and seemingly inflexible. That's why we need the Lord's help to redeem our use of time.

Schedules

If a man is to respond to his call as a leader of people, he must arrange his life into the proper balance of essential, important, and ordinary activities. In short, a father needs a schedule. For me, a schedule was a giant hurdle that took me a long time to clear. For many years I had allowed the demands of my business to establish my schedule, adjusting my personal and family life to suit my work. Today, God has led me to reverse these priorities. Little by little I was able to take control over the pace of my life.

I do not want to propose a specific schedule, but, based on my experience, to simply suggest the items which a man should consider in ordering his day and his week. The first hurdles to overcome are extreme attitudes toward schedules. Some people resist a structured life altogether; others make a schedule an end in itself. Both extremes are dangerous. Although most men need a schedule to fulfill their responsibilities, they miss its purpose. For a Christian father, schedules are tools to help us love and serve others.

The schedule God wants for us will put him first, our primary relationships and other human priorities next, and ourselves behind both. The specifics of a schedule will vary with each man, but the objective and the framework is the same. It facilitates our love of God and of others. The structure of our lives must bear fruit in our highest priorities.

One benefit which a good schedule yields is that we learn how to do ordinary things more quickly in order to have more time for the extraordinary. Where most men are exhausted at the end of a workday, God wants our work and routine tasks done faster and more easily so we can enjoy our families.

A change of this kind took place in our home a few years ago. We were always starting the day off-balance. I allowed just enough time each morning to prepare personally for work. Anna had to get several children up and dressed, cook breakfast, and supervise the preparation of lunches. Mornings were confusing, anxious, high-pressure times. As we watched our children leave the house in the same harried state each morning, we knew God wanted a change.

Most changes in a Christian home begin with the head of that home. In our case, hunger for peace motivated me to take the initiative. I prayed about changing our mornings and also asked Anna for help. Over the months, a new schedule slowly began to emerge. That new pattern began with me, it flowed to

Anna, and eventually it took hold of the entire family.

The key was a decision on my part to change. I began rising one hour before my family for personal prayer, exercise, and a shower. Anna responded by setting an attractive breakfast table the night before. The children cooperated by making their lunches for the week on Sunday and freezing them. We discovered how to zip through the ordinary and the routine quickly, in order to be ready for the extraordinary.

This might seem like a small change, but it greatly strengthened our family. It enabled us to begin our day as a family in prayer, then eat a peaceful meal together. We began to experience our mornings together as a time to "put on the armor." For a Christian family, this means starting a day together with prayer, the Word, and a meal. We are then ready to go out into a world which is not necessarily supportive of our Christian ideals.

A schedule should arrange our priorities while allowing enough free time to respond to "the surprises of the Spirit." It can help settle our pace and also improve the quality of our lives. As a Christian family, our goal is to live a life which is discernably different than the world around us, and to draw others into that life because of its fruit.

Creative schedules will allow time to respond to people who are hungry for Jesus. When we live in God's order, others will ask how we do it. We can tell them the answer—our families are different because Jesus is Lord of our homes. When our normal tasks can be done efficiently, with a pleasant attitude and at God's pace, we have room left to respond in love to whatever or whomever enters our life that day.

Schedules should be planned carefully and viewed flexibly. I construct our family schedule in two steps: First, a daily routine, then weekly events fitted into specific time blocks. As our service to Christians outside our family increases, safe limits should be established to prevent these activities from weakening our home life in the very same way worldly distractions previously had done.

No schedule should become an end in itself. It is a means; the end is the freedom we are promised as sons of God. We should control our schedules and not allow them to control us. We can fall into bondage to the very thing which God has provided in order to free us.

A tightly planned schedule can control us in two ways. First, it can deceive us into trying to "do" more than we should. It can help us pack our lives full of things we possibly shouldn't be doing. A schedule can present the same hazard that modern kitchen appliances often do. Rather than allowing the machine to order life at a manageable pace, many women use the extra time the machine provides to do other work. They end up more exhausted than they would if they didn't have the appliance. The second pitfall is to view the specifics of the schedule so rigidly that we fail to see and respond to a critical need. Like any structure, a schedule is created to serve people. When it fails to do that, we must change it or drop it, always choosing to do the loving thing, not just the scheduled thing.

Control your schedule, constantly evaluating it in terms of its original objectives. Look for the life of peace, joy, and love which has enough room for evangelization, effective service to others, recreation, and free time. Let your schedule provide for you with fullness, not bondage.

No father should try to make a schedule without help. Pray about it. Ask your wife and even your children what they think. The schedule must work for the common good. Consult another father who has had experience with a schedule. When you've collected the best wisdom you can find, test it and don't be afraid to experiment. You shouldn't be satisfied with any plan just because it seems good. It can get better.

Being Busy and Looking Busy

Busyness has become a way of life in our world of work. Many men really are busy. Some of these busy men desire to look busy because it makes them feel important.

This became clear when I started commuting to New York a day or two a week to make sales calls on top executives. I had previously worked with men whose lives were hectic. Now, in New York, the atmosphere was truly frantic, almost overpowering. You could feel the pressure as soon as the train stopped at Penn Station. It would get worse throughout the day. Important clients would cancel appointments which I had worked weeks to get. Most men were so busy that their phone calls were screened by secretaries who would only put through the highest priority calls. Gradually my pace increased to keep up with the pack, and soon I was acting as busy as everyone else. Collapsing into my train seat at night, I had no energy or desire left for anyone. Despite my attempts at study, many nights I could only fall asleep.

Those painful days in New York taught me some valuable lessons about being busy and looking busy. These lessons can be applied to Christian fatherhood. In New York I watched high level executives accomplish large amounts of work and deal with many people in a short span of time. They actually spent fewer hours in the office than many people who look very busy. The average New York executive arrives at work by 9:30, takes one to two hours for lunch and leaves by 5:00 or 5:30. How did they accomplish what they had to? Here is their secret: They did their personal work some other time, leaving their prime office time available for managing other people and seeking new business. Every good executive must be able to do this. He must sacrifice his personal time in order to be fully available to others during the business day. The able executive doesn't appear to be interrupted when someone arrives for an appointment. He's already done his work for the meeting and he's ready to focus on the person he is meeting with. The top executives I met had mastered one important principle of leading people: *They were fully present to others.*

Presence

To be present to another is to be physically, mentally, and emotionally available to them. It means concentrating on what others are saying and being open to change our opinions based on what that person has to say. Our presence resists "looking busy" to impress others, and aims at making the other person feel like he or she *is* the most important person for us at that time. Presence is a learned art; it involves some dying to self and it is a key to leadership of people.

During eighteen years in a major construction firm, I saw many examples of good and bad leaders. I measured their ability by their capacity to be present to others. Everyone suffers when the leader is preoccupied with other things. A man who has to "look busy" is constantly pre-occupied. He can't relax, unwind—or listen.

As our company became more prosperous, we were able to attract and train better executives and managers. During recent years, I was especially pleased with the management team which developed. We emphasized the managers' ability to make subordinates feel relaxed and important when speaking to them. The men in charge work at home on the little time-consuming tasks which are part of every business. They arrive at the office early to clear the mail and to dictate letters. Then they are ready to respond to those new problems or opportunities that day presents. These men are able to cultivate the major asset of any company—its people.

The art of presence is important at work, but it's critical in a Christian home. Wives and children are frustrated when they cannot communicate with a father who is too busy at work or has learned how to always look that way. A man must learn how to discipline his life, and especially his time, to allow himself to be present to his family. A child quickly learns that Daddy is too tired or too busy to pay attention to him and will look for someone else to relate to. His father, God's primary channel of grace, was unfortunately not available.

If you think I'm exaggerating the dangers of a father's busyness, let me give you some disturbing statistics. A study I saw recently shows that the average American father spends about thirty-seven seconds per day with his child. It also commented on the importance of children perceiving that they are loved through the time that we spend with them. It gets down to simple truths: Our families need quality time and they need a father who is present.

The pressures leading to fathers' mental and emotional separation from their families do not come just from the world of careers and occupations. We can get just as badly out of focus in the Lord's work. I've had enough experience with the potential dangers of "holy busyness" to speak with authority about the matter. I have seen the same symptoms of busyness in fathers who are preoccupied with the details of ministry, service organizations, and community problems. The reason for the lack of presence at home may be "holier," but the effect is the same. Fathers can be out night after night at meetings, getting so deeply enmeshed in the lives of brothers and sisters in the Lord, that they neglect their families. We can get so involved in the Lord's work that we can actually miss the Lord.

Ego, pride, ambition, or other motives can draw us away from our principal call as fathers. This truth surfaced for me when I drew back from my career to begin work on this book. At first, I moved into my new task with a good sense of balance. However, the practical demands of writing soon started to mount and the book began to preoccupy me. I found myself faced with a basic decision: Was I going to write about fatherhood or be a father? In essence, the book gave me a new reason not to be present to my family. This meant looking at my priorities again, very candidly. Thanks to give and take with Anna, I never got too far off balance, but the pull was there and it's there for everyone. That pull is not from the Holy Spirit; grace and truth are needed to fight it.

Sabbaticals

When our lives are balanced, we can work hard without becoming exhausted. But there are times when all of us get drained physically, spiritually, mentally, and emotionally. We become like a good field which is overworked after producing excellent crops season after season. The Lord gave the answer to this problem when he told the Israelites, "When you enter the land that I am giving you, let the land, too, keep a sabbath for the Lord. For six years you may sow your field, and for six years prune your vineyard, gathering in their produce. But during the seventh year, the land shall have a complete rest, a sabbath for the Lord, when you may neither sow your field nor prune your vineyard" (Lv 25:1-4).

We should apply the same wisdom to ourselves. There are times when we need a sabbatical—a period of rest to fight the busyness of modern life. Our rest doesn't have to be a year off; instead it can take the form of a change of pace, a time when we do nothing "important" for a while. A rest like this can be especially valuable when we are heavily committed to serving other people in addition to our family and our work. The leader of a renewal activity or the pastor of a congregation may get to a point of simply being "out of grace." When this happens, he has to step back and let Jesus love him in a special way for a time.

A sabbatical for a busy father may mean simply cutting back outside activities to allow time to enjoy his children, or it may require a vacation. We are weak vessels and our clay feet stick out when we're tired. Don't be afraid to say "no" and let your field rest for a while. When the Spirit stirs you back into activity, you will produce a more abundant harvest.

It is also important to keep the weekly Sabbath as a time of rest and refreshment. Our Sundays should be family days when we try to be together as much as possible. We need to resist the lure of unnecessary tasks or activities, and instead emphasize ways to build our togetherness. Don't follow the world's example and use Sunday to work and shop. God in his wisdom has given us the correct pace: Six days shall you labor, but the Sabbath is set aside for God.

Managing Your Time

In discovering how to invest our time for the Kingdom of God, we must first concede the necessity of living in the modern world. Few of us are being called to a monastic isolation or to life in a simple agrarian culture. As Christians, we are called to be "in the world but not of it." I'd like to propose a few creative suggestions which helped me achieve the balance to live this way. These are not solutions for major problems, but are more like preventive maintenance to forestall exhaustion. If we can learn little ways of slowing down, the Spirit will be able to guide us around most major obstacles. Many of these suggestions draw on wisdom from the monastic life. My occasional visits to religious communities have taught me some ways to bring peace to my life.

Unplanned Time

The Benedictines at Mt. Saviour in Elmira, New York are a holy family, living a very simple yet deeply spiritual and active life. They pray, work, eat, and rest in scheduled intervals throughout the day. Yet these monks firmly believe that free time is necessary to build a contemplative spirituality. They would say, "You've got to learn how to waste time, conscientiously." That sounded foolish at first, until I began to see how it worked in their lives.

Fathers leading active families in a modern society should learn how to "waste" some time with their families and to do it with grace. We should have unplanned free time. It can also take the form of quiet time, when everyone in the house is alone and at peace. A human being needs to learn how to be at peace with himself and his God aside from scheduled activities.

As a family, we've used this technique to accomplish "unplanned vacations." We will just decide to take off and go nowhere in particular. We use our home as a motel and return only to sleep. We visit friends and tourist attractions—anything that strikes our fancy. The children love this approach because it has a sense of adventure to it. An unplanned vacation doesn't take a lot of money and it builds lasting memories. When the kids talk about the high points of our summer, they will invariably remember those times when we were together and just "wasted" some time.

Wasting time with someone makes them a priority for us. That person feels important because we were willing to break our pattern and just "be" with them. This is critical for a husband and wife. We can get so wrapped up in loving other people that we can forget how much we need to love each other. A period of time invested in doing nothing together can be just the right tonic for a tired Christian mother and father.

Mini-Retreats

Another little insight which came from the Benedictines at Mt. Saviour is the need for mini-retreats. They've discovered that even a holy man of God living in a monastery must have a change in scenery. The monks call this "Laxo." It does not have to be a major spiritual excursion, but more of an impromptu, simple refresher which you can work into your normal schedule.

I take Laxo by going to a favorite spot within one hour from my home, and simply enjoy being there. This kind of breather restores me physically, spiritually, and emotionally. It's a good idea to return to the same spot, but you can also look around for new ones. When traveling on business, I would look for a quiet park to sit in for fifteen to twenty minutes between meetings. Most people find the beauty of the mountains or the seashore are perfect, if they are accessible. The chapel and grounds of a monastery, a convent, or a retreat center are other favorite spots. Religious communities are usually receptive to people who need some peace and quiet.

The whole key to Laxo for me is being able to do it within a normal schedule and not having to plan too far in advance.

Short prayer

Another useful tool is an adaptation of the short times of prayer which religious communities practice throughout the day. I can't join an order for matins and vespers, but I can take brief periods during the day for "prayer breaks." As my prayer life deepens, the need is growing for prayerful contact with the Spirit more often than once a day. Sometimes, my prayer breaks are active—loud times of verbal prayer. Others might be more reflective, quieter times. All that's needed is a private spot where I can give thanks and praise to God at intervals during the day. It might be the car, in the shower, an open field, or a parking lot. If you look, you will find a place to praise the Lord with enthusiasm. Also, you may want to share some of these times with Christian friends. St. Paul said, "Pray at all times, in the Spirit."

Praise breaks will help you fight off confusion and exhaustion. The psalmist wrote, "Out of the mouths of babes and sucklings, you have fashioned praise because of your foes, to silence the hostile and the vengeful" (Ps 8:3). This referred to flesh and blood enemies, but we can use the same weapon against emotional forces. When you find yourself laboring in a difficult situation, consider a prayer break. Sometimes a shift in attention back to the Lord is just what you need.

Measuring Priorities

Another technique I have learned is to use the yardstick of time to measure priorities. That means if something is as important as we claim it is, let's put our time where our claim is! A scale you might use is a principle which I've called "halving."

The principle of halving suggests that the highest priorities of our lives—God and family—should get no less than half of our available time. Time is God's gift to us. We should give at least half of it back to him. This principle has a lot of scriptural basis. Consider the story of Zacchaeus, the tax collector who received Jesus. When onlookers called him a sinner, Zacchaeus said this to defend himself: "I give half my belongings, Lord, to the poor. If I have defrauded anyone in the least, I pay him back fourfold" (Lk 19:8). Zacchaeus didn't "buy" salvation that day, yet his response to it was a tangible one.

The scriptures also tell the story of Tobit and his wife Anna. Tobit was a Jew who was deported to Nineveh after the fall of the northern kingdom of Israel in 721 B.C. In the midst of terrible ordeals, including blindness, he sent his son to far-off Media to bring back a large amount of money which he had left there. The Lord intervened in miraculous ways to save Tobit's son and his daughter-in-law; eventually God healed his blindness. To praise God, Tobit also gave away half of his treasure.

Our treasure is time. It is a gift we *can* choose to give away.

I'm using the halving principle as a guideline to insure that my focus is on the Kingdom of God and my family. When working on my schedule, I add the time up in various categories. If it begins to exceed that spent on my first priorities, a change is needed in the schedule.

This balance, in fact, is built into the way of life of the Norbertine order of priests. Their founder, St. Norbert, was called to a mission of renewal for the secular priesthood in twelfth century Europe. His rule was that his canons would spend six months in the monastic cloister to deepen in the spiritual life and then six months out in the world to preach and serve the poor.

Many married laymen, involved in full time Christian service do something similar. One busy man I know puts it this way: "Three nights out, three nights home, and one to rest." This is the kind of balance which God wants fathers to achieve in their lives.

Switching Gears

Many men have trouble separating themselves mentally and emotionally from their jobs so that they can arrive home free to offer quality time to their loved ones. Sometimes worries about work spoil whole evenings and weekends which should be devoted to wives and children. Instead of being present, Daddy has a "far away" look on his face.

Ed, a friend of mine who is a traveling salesman, has an effective way to switch gears. To phase out of his business day, he stops at the park and prays for ten minutes before going home. The break in the normal pattern and the refreshment of ten minutes of prayer allows him to shed his work problems and walk into the house with a smile. This works for me too. I also suggest not bringing0 work home with you. A loaded briefcase in the house can exert a powerful tug on your thoughts.

Tolstoy grasped an insight for the use of time in his novel *War and Peace*. Pierre, a restless young poet goes off to war. He discovers something about the meaning of life as he is being nursed back to health in a prison camp. A starving man shares his last potato with Pierre. The truth emerges: "The most important thing in life is the living of it."

The balance which God wants for all fathers is a healthy mixture of wholeness and holiness. That balance can become real in your life as you learn how to invest the treasure of your time.

CHAPTER NINE

Simplicity:
Our Use of Resources

The second key to personal maturity in Christ is a new simplicity in our lifestyle. If we are to become God's men, we must deal with the general complexity in and around us.

My own lack of simplicity stems from materialism which in turn is rooted in my childhood. I was born during the Depression, to lower-income parents. In the Thirties, the birth of a child meant serious considerations for a family. My earliest memories include a concern for physical necessities. Would we have enough to eat? Would there be coal this winter? Could we make the mortgage payments? The primary concern was survival. By many standards my family was poor, yet we were very materialistic. Our identity was found in what we possessed, not our personhood. This preoccupation with goods complicates the lives of both the rich, who trust in the wealth they have, and the poor, who place faith in what they hope to have.

My upbringing gave me a strong desire for material security, and, as an adult, I sought to acquire more things. As a young man, a higher income relieved my insecurity, but only for a while. What seemed like an energetic drive for business success was really an attempt to achieve financial independence and thus relieve my fears. This was my inner drive when I met the Lord and felt his unconditional love for the first time. His love cracked my shell of fear and insecurity. I was filled with a warmth which flowed from a heart that loved me for who I was, not for what I could accomplish.

As my relationship with Jesus deepened, I experienced a growing hunger for a simpler style of life. Persevering in prayer, I was drawn to the stories in Matthew's Gospel on the danger of riches. "If you seek perfection, go, sell your possessions, and give to the poor. I assure you, only with difficulty will a rich man enter into the Kingdom of God. I repeat what I said: It is easier for a camel to pass through a needle's eye than for a rich man to enter the Kingdom of God" (Mt 19:21-24). I could see myself in those parables. I was the rich young man who was clutching on to things. The fears of not having enough had led me to acquire more and more and more. Paradoxically, the more I acquired, the more complex my life became. The things I had and wanted were becoming a serious obstacle to my response to the Lord.

In reflecting on this dilemma and sharing it with friends, a vision began to form in my mind. I could see a beautiful field with rich lush foliage, fed by a stream of sparkling clear water. The water in that stream obviously had a special quality to it because everything which the stream touched was healthy and beautiful. I approached the field and noticed it was enclosed by a fence which had only one gate. I saw myself standing in front of the gate, my arms filled with empty pots. I wanted to enter by the gate and go to the stream. But, like the camel and the rich young man in the gospel, I was too heavily laden. Those pots, which represented my plan for capturing some of that wonderful water, kept me from passing through the gate. To pass into this new territory, I had to drop those things which appeared so necessary. The simplicity which God wants means dropping the empty pots we've collected in the pastures of the world.

We're being called to shift our attention away from things and achievements toward God and other people. As we develop new ways of feeling, thinking, and acting, we can begin to experience the richness of God's Kingdom. The Father wants us to bathe in his care, seeing that all we possess is a gift from him. We don't own anything; everything, including ourselves, belongs to Jesus. We are called to be stewards, trustees of God's wealth, responsible for wisely investing our material, intellectual, emotional and spiritual resources. These are his gifts to us. We are joint heirs with the Son, "Just as all that belongs to me is yours, so all that belongs to you is mine" (Jn 17:10).

The Simplicity of Jesus

The simplicity of Jesus' life poses a constant challenge to the hard and barren soil of our possessive attitudes. He gives us the Father's perspective on those patterns which complicate our lives. Jesus came to us in the humblest of settings. Contrast the circumstances of his birth with the way we Americans celebrate it. In giving gifts to each other at Christmas, we wrap ordinary things in expensive paper to exalt the importance of the package's contents. By contrast, Jesus, the most precious gift of all, came in the most common wrapping possible—a naked baby in a manger.

Everything about the circumstances and the setting of our Savior's coming reveals its essential simplicity. God did not wait to send his Son until man had created a technological society of mass media, computers, and jet travel. Instead his Son was born in a stable in the farthest outpost of the Roman Empire. The comfortable and the satisfied were absent from the drama at Bethlehem. Those who surrounded Jesus' birth were simple people: Mary, Joseph, the innkeeper, and especially the shepherds who saw and recognized the star which foretold his birth. These people were simple enough to actually believe that God would enter into time in such a humble way.

Jesus led a simple life. He worked with his stepfather Joseph in Nazareth as a carpenter. He used his hands in a demanding trade. We can identify with a God who cares enough for those around him to provide for their material support. He worked most of those years in quiet obscurity. This is not a glorious wrapping for the Son of God, but more of the plain, flesh-colored covering which the Father chose for his treasure.

The gospel which Jesus preached is filled with little stories about ordinary life. His words have been translated and analyzed by intelligent men for two thousand years, but the words

remain simple and the message is clear: "Come follow me."
Jesus is asking us to pattern our lives after his example. What a
challenge for modern man! We are to imitate someone who
lived simply by the principle of unconditional love.

The gospel often speaks of repentance and pays considerable
attention to the dangers of material wealth and possessions.
The call to simplify our lives is stated repeatedly. Jesus doesn't
call all of us to material poverty, but he does clearly identify
material goods as a major cause for our separation from God
and our fellowman. We hold onto our resources so tightly and
worry about them so much that we cannot fully embrace others
or even Jesus himself.

Being a practical teacher, Jesus taught us about the dangers
in our possessions, but he also met people's pressing personal
needs. He addressed human suffering with food, healing, and
forgiveness of sins. In the gospel accounts, Jesus always meets
someone's deepest need first, before he reveals himself as the
Son of God. He could have captured us by his might and
power. Instead, he came among us as a servant.

The servant Jesus was concerned for everyone except himself. He possessed no thing and no person, but embraced
everything he received as a gift. "Though he was in the form
of God, he did not deem equality with God something to be
grasped at. Rather, he emptied himself and took the form of a
slave, being born in the likeness of man. He was known to be
of human estate, and it was thus that he humbled himself,
obediently accepting even death, death on a cross!"
(Phil 2:6-8).

Materialism

The simplicity of Jesus stands in sharp contrast to modern
materialism, which demands constant concern with what we
have or don't have. Materialism is a vice and like a vise: Its
jaws continually tighten around us. We can temporarily relieve
the pressure by some new acquisition. But the pressure is only
eased; it's never eliminated. When we give in to materialism,
we never have enough.

It has taken many years for me to break free from those jaws; still temptation lingers. It's a pain which is known by all—rich, middle class, and poor. Fathers can only break the grip of materialism when we make a clear decision to fight it. With hope in the Lord's power, we can offer our children a better way.

Materialism blurs the distinction between our needs and our wants. Jesus promised that God will provide all our needs. However, many of us become disillusioned because we are praying for our wants. Of course, the Lord wants more for us than the bare necessities, but we can't be truly grateful for that abundance unless we know what we actually *need*.

Most of us have trouble separating our wants from our needs because of modern advertising which tries to get us to acquire things we don't need. It's a powerful tool and it works. Take note to watch the effect of advertising on your children after Thanksgiving. The ads for toys create a mystique; they are seeds which blossom into large flowers of desire. The futility of this desire is evident on Christmas morning when the child gets the real toy. That which was wrapped so brightly and advertised so well is exposed for what it really is—often disappointing and seldom reaching their expectations.

We all need a lot of training to distinguish between needs and wants. Periodically, everyone in our home lists their needs on paper. It's interesting to watch a child review what he or she already has and then discard a number of tempting desires as not really necessary. This exercise leaves us with a good sense of our true needs. We can't begin to teach our children this kind of discernment too early.

Another tool of materialism is the harmless looking piece of indented plastic we call a credit card. The only credit which these cards offer is to the marketing genius of American retailers. We live in a "buy-now" society. The credit system suggests instant satisfaction, but provides frustration at the end of each month when the bills roll in. Instant credit deprives us of the satisfaction of dreaming and saving for something which we should have. The real joy of acquiring some new piece of furniture or appliance should begin as we struggle to save up enough to finally buy it.

Liberal use of credit cards can seriously damage a family's budget. There is the possibility it can damage the nation's economy as well. The figures are staggering. *Newsweek* magazine ended an article on consumer debt with the comment that, "The American consumer lives on borrowed money—and the gnawing fear is that the economy may be living on borrowed time as a result."

Over the last few years my income has fallen as I have taken on new work for the Lord. When my income fell below the level of our previously budgeted expenses, I had to learn new consumer techniques. Other Christian fathers who were trying to simplify their lives advised me to eliminate credit cards altogether. I still use them for some travel, but I've been able to jetison most of our plastic timebombs. Today we buy with cash. If there isn't any, we wait. Resisting future debt may not work for everyone, but for me it has meant a new freedom. We felt this freedom with special intensity as we completed our first Christmas which was addressed with prayerful discernment and cash purchases. We bought less, but we enjoyed the season more.

A simpler life also seems to be a happier, healthier life. When the media formed my attitudes and opinions, I used to feel frustration regarding the world's problems. Any effort on my part seemed like a hopeless gesture. However, as my life got simpler, especially regarding media, I began to see how we could affect others in truly significant ways. For example, we changed our family's eating habits as a result of reading literature published by *Bread for the World*, a Christian organization concerned about world hunger. Since the grain used to fatten our steaks is needed to keep human beings alive, we cut down on our intake of red meat. The decision to simplify our diet has led to others; we try to bake our own bread, eat more balanced meals, and take better care of ourselves. Moving with God's plan for simplicity has many blessings for a family.

The word of God challenges us to eliminate our excesses and simplify our lives. Materialism is the external manifestation of one of the darker desires of the human heart: the love of money and the independence it promises. Nothing is more devious and powerful, and nothing can distract us from the Kingdom of God more thoroughly.

Stewardship of Resources

The Christian father is a good steward of all his human and spiritual resources. What does that mean? It is a quality that should mark our attitude toward everything God has placed in our care. In the New Testament, the words "steward" and "stewardship" are closely related to our word "economy." The root meaning is management of a household. A steward, therefore, is one who manages a household. A steward was a trusted servant whom the master appointed to administer his holdings, giving him a broad range of responsibilities and powers with which to carry out his function.

A concise explanation of our call to stewardship is given by the National Catholic Stewardship Council:

Stewardship is the wise and respectful use of the gifts of God's loving creation. Its goal is to recognize profoundly that creation is in man's trust, and that we must respond by managing justly his precious treasures. We do this by adopting a simple lifestyle, free of excess materialism, that shares love and self.

There are three clear signs of stewardship as the New Testament describes it. First, it always refers to the care of *another's* wealth; the steward never has his own possessions. As Christians, we belong totally to God; we don't even own ourselves. "You are not your own. You have been purchased, and at a price. So glorify God in your body" (1 Cor 6:19-20). We are trusted servants; all that we are and possess comes from God. We have a responsibility to lovingly and carefully administer God's wealth in faith and obedience.

The second important feature of Christian stewardship lies in the relationship of steward and master. We are the steward, the servant; God is the master. We should never forget this.

The steward is not giving to God only his "fair share" of possessions. He does God's bidding—knowing who the master is.

The third characteristic of stewardship is that the New Testament primarily focuses on truth and spiritual gifts—not on material goods (1 Cor 4:1-5; Col 1:25; 1 Pt 4:10). Spiritual gifts and graces are the main part of the treasures which are in our care.

A handy way to look at the resources which have been entrusted to us is to remember "the three T's"—Time, Treasures, and Talents. I discussed the use of our time in chapter eight. Here I'll discuss stewardship over the remaining two T's—Treasures and Talents.

Treasures

The Lord called me to personal stewardship when my income was high and an affluent lifestyle was a real temptation. I realized that God had allowed me to experience some material security, not just to relieve the fears of poverty stemming from my childhood, but also as a holy trust which I would have to account for at a later date. I came to see that I had to manage both my talents and my treasures in preparation for deeper service to God. Images of Joseph came to me—Joseph the Pharaoh's servant, stewarding grain for eventual use by his own family during hard times which were to come. "(Pharoah) took a liking to Joseph and made him his personal attendant; he put him in charge of his household and entrusted to him all his possessions. From the moment that he put him in charge of his household and all his possessions, the Lord blessed the Egyptian's house for Joseph's sake; in fact, the Lord's blessing was on everything he owned, both inside the house and out. Having left everything he owned in Joseph's charge, he gave no thought, with Joseph there, to anything but the food he ate" (Gn 39:4-6).

I realized God had entrusted much into my care and had given me a special responsibility. My response was to simplify my personal style of life and to reduce our household expenses. This was done at a time when my income was high and we were able to "store grain" for later use. Eventually this act of stewardship permitted me more time to serve the Church directly—including the time to write this book.

Our concrete decisions about the use of material goods are influenced mostly by the priorities which we have established for ourselves. If our priorities reflect God's order, we will allocate our resources to reinforce those priorities. We may think that pressing circumstances determine how we invest our time, talent, and treasures, but the goals and ideals in our mind and heart usually determine these choices.

This principle operates most clearly when you have to decide how to spend some extra money. What would you do with a bonus check, a tax refund, or perhaps lottery winnings? The motivation behind your life becomes clearer when you must make a decision like this. Would you put that money to use serving those whom God has placed in your care, or would you quietly stash it away for some personal fantasy? Would you seek God's will in these decisions?

Being a faithful steward of God's treasures is not an option for a Christian father. It is a command. God will not ask our wives to account for the resources he placed in our families. He will ask us. The Father has given us much, and much will be expected. The gospels speak clearly about this, even though we may try to pass over these words. A good example is the parable of the silver pieces (Mt 25:14-30).

The task of wise stewardship is to use our resources for the Kingdom of God. This means that we can be neither foolishly extravagant nor fearfully protective. Consider Jesus' parable of the rich man who had enjoyed a good harvest. "'What shall I do?' he asked himself. 'I have no place to store my harvest. I know!' he said. 'I will pull down my grain bins and build larger ones. All my grain and my goods will go there. Then I will say to myself: You have blessings in reserve for years to come. Relax! Eat heartily, drink well. Enjoy yourself.' But God said to him, 'You fool! This very night your life shall be required of you. To whom will all this piled-up wealth of yours go?' That is the way it works with the man who grows rich for himself instead of growing rich in the sight of God" (Lk 12:17-21).

Talents

Although we are spiritual men of God, we still have talents which need tangible expression, especially in our secular employment. We must work to provide for our families. God has given us the strength and the talent needed to materially support the life placed in our care. Living a spiritual life does not mean living in a daydream, expecting God to do for us what we are unwilling to do for ourselves. Life in Christ does not eliminate our responsibility and initiative in the secular world, but instead involves a deeper understanding of our work as a holy thing.

The Church has always put a high value on a man's labor. To restate that position, this sentence was included in the Constitution on the Church published after the Second Vatican Council. "By means of their daily work, they should climb to the heights of holiness, which is indeed apostolic" (Const. Church, Chapter V, Sec. 42). In our age, where the value of human labor can be lost or underrated, prayerful men drafting a document on the Church wanted laymen to know that their work is holy and precious in the eyes of God.

With the coming of Jesus, God fully immersed himself in the human condition and shouldered every aspect of life—including work. Joseph of Nazareth worked to support Jesus and Mary. Jesus also worked—at a strenuous and exacting trade. The Son of God toiled with wood, sweating to create needed tools and equipment. He learned how to fashion benches, tables, and also yokes. Jesus must have learned a great deal about yokes, for these had to be individually fitted to the shoulders of oxen and horses to prevent chaffing and abrasion. The memory of that perfect fit was undoubtedly in his mind when he told us to be yoked to him. The yoke which Jesus offers is just right for us. We can pull any worldly burden, because Jesus is helping to carry most of the load.

God gives us talents to use in our work, but often a job can consume a man's life or even tempt him to compromise his faith. The pressure of work can distort a man's perspective and push him into allowing worldly standards to establish his criteria for behavior. The excuse, "Everyone else is doing it; why can't I?" is a dangerous rationalization which can lead to sin. A Christian father is often called to be a contradiction to modern norms in an office or a factory. He should be a sign of wholeness and holiness for other men, an example to point them toward something beyond what they now struggle with. Jesus did not call us to be "one of the boys" or "nice guys." He called us to be men of God who stand up for what is right and just, even if it is not in fashion. We do not have the option to deny Jesus' Lordship, even at work. If your stance for God cannot fit into your secular employment, the choice is clear: Pray seriously about changing your job!

The pain of denying the Lord in an environment loaded with sin can be intense. The apostle Peter knew this anguish and it must have lingered with him throughout his life. "Simon, Simon! Remember that Satan has asked for you, to sift you all like wheat. But I have prayed for you that your faith may never fail. You in turn must strengthen your brothers" (Lk 22:31-32). We will be sifted too, but Jesus' prayer will sustain us and bring us courage.

The action of the Holy Spirit in a man and his family is creative and often unexpected, producing an abundance of new discoveries. Some of those coming forth in my family are the undiscovered gifts and talents which lie dormant in all of us. In our home we've seen singing, music, painting, gardening, needlework, creative writing and many other hidden talents come out as we continue to turn our lives over to Jesus. We've also seen existing skills like cooking and baking take on new creative dimensions which move them out of the category of chores.

Similar things have happened to others I know. An example is my friend John Bonella, the father of five children. John has a marketing and sales background; he works diligently at his job. However, over the past few years surprising creativity has blossomed from his home workshop. He is active in painting, model making, wood carving, sculpting, and beautiful modifications to his home. His children are following suit. Where did all this come from? Not from his education or his background.

John simply has allowed the Lord to bring out the natural skills and talents stored within. The same thing is happening to many of the Christian men I know.

This creative wave seems to include a rediscovery of old ways of doing things. The energy crisis and tight money should spur a Christian father to display his creativity. My friends and I have been rediscovering the richness and wisdom of manual labor. Before, many men would take out a loan and hire a contractor to repair their home. Today, Christian men are working together on each other's homes to share and develop their skills. This saves money, frees us from the need for high income, gives men genuine pride in accomplishment, and provides a healthy release from the intense pressure of daily work.

One of the occasions for discovering my hidden talents has been through wholesome recreation. As a family, with ages ranging from six into the forties, it takes some creativity to play and have a lot of fun together.

The first thing I realized is that fun time doesn't just happen; it must be seen as a priority and then planned for. This was part of the overall simplification of my life. Children should experience their father in all dimensions of life, before his God on his knees and also in shorts romping like a child in the Kingdom. Growing in relationship with Jesus shouldn't create a somber spirit in a man, but rather a spirit which seeks to celebrate all of life. Today, as my work becomes more demanding, the need to be able to relax and "let it all hang out" is critical. When I begin to take myself too seriously, a family wrestling match or volley ball game will usually bring me back into focus.

Although sports are a fine way to unwind and have some fun together, there is always the danger of excessive competition. The goal of fun time is to relax—not to compete against ourselves or others. In the body of Christ, we're not pitted against each other; we run the race together. Each part is necessary to insure that the whole body reaches the finish line. Excess competition is a manifestation of our root sin of pride, our desire to be number one. We often have to take special steps to avoid stirring up our pride when we have fun together. With Jesus, he's number one and we're all trying harder.

I have a particular tendency to take myself too seriously and become very competitive when I'm overworked and not rested. To balance my weaknesses, I have come to rely on other families for a balanced approach. As my Christian friends see me getting too serious, they know it's time for some fun. I've begun to take this to heart.

One specific step we have taken is to invest in good recreation equipment to allow our home to become a place where our family can play together in simple and inexpensive ways. For example, a volley ball or badminton net, a basketball backboard and hoop, some softball equipment, etc. will insure that the children can find some fun at home and will see their Dad and Mom together enjoying themselves. The sporting equipment has also led us to clarify how a group of Christians should play without excessive competition. Family recreation doesn't have to cost very much. There are plenty of games which can be borrowed from the local library or purchased inexpensively. Whatever your choice, just enjoy some time together and relax.

As the foundations of family life are strengthened, we can be brought to a point of asking the deeper questions about our talents. Each man of God must eventually ask, "Lord, where am I going? What do you want me to do with the natural, material and spiritual resources you've given to me? Am I using what you've given to build your Kingdom?" These are not idle questions. Mature Christian men ask them as a natural outgrowth of their deepening relationships with Jesus.

I have gained a few insights into these questions through struggles with them myself. Most of the time these questions do not mean that the Lord is calling for a complete break with the past. For most men, the search for God's perfect will leads to a0 realization and completion of what already is. In other words, don't disregard what you're doing as insignificant. Be thankful for where you are and keep listening for the voice of the Shepherd leading you to what will be.

Another truth about God's future for us is that his plan will not contradict our natural talents and gifts. His perfect will is the most natural course, the most productive, and the one that brings the most peace and joy. Grace, God's life in us, builds on our natural qualities. It doesn't come in some strange new way which would reverse the good which is already operating in us. We should not look for some totally new gift or a strange talent to emerge and signal a radical departure into his perfect plan. We've all been given an abundance of gift, talent, and strength. The Father expects that we will learn how to use that in building his Kingdom. "When much has been given a man, much will be required of him. More will be asked of a man to whom more has been entrusted" (Lk 12:48).

Tithing

Although the children of God have freely received a full inheritance of the Kingdom, we seem to have a problem of clutching onto our treasures too tightly. God wants us to learn how to loosen our grip on resources, seeing all as gift, to be used at his direction.

A visual example of finding the right grip was depicted in the recent movie of the classic "Superman" story. Superman invites the astounded Lois Lane to come fly with him over the city of Metropolis. Before she can catch her breath, they're soaring in the clouds. Lois is flying—but how? She's clutching onto Superman for dear life and the beauty of the experience is lost in her fear of falling. As the musical tempo builds, Lois slips down to the tip of Superman's fingers and with the grace of an eagle begins to soar with her hero. We all need to acquire that kind of grip: firm, yet gentle.

The Father wants us to approach our material resources freely, in a way that is guided by his Spirit. The tool given by the Father to teach us is the regular practice of tithing. Tithing is the voluntary giving of some part of what we have back to God from whom it came.

In the Old Testament, tithing was part of the Law. The Jewish people were taught from the earliest time to bring offerings and sacrifices to God and to return ten percent of their resources to the Lord. However, the legal aspects of this prescription, more than their love of God, came to guide their motives.

The New Testament teaches us something different: All our resources belong to the Lord, not just ten percent of them. We are stewards over what the Lord has given us. Above all, God is concerned about the condition of our hearts rather than the amount or the way we give. God wants more than obedience to the Law; he wants willing obedience and cheerful sons. "Let me say this much: He who sows sparingly will reap sparingly, and he who sows bountifully will reap bountifully. Everyone must give according to what he has inwardly decided; not sadly, not grudgingly, for God loves a cheerful giver" (2 Cor 9:6-7).

The voluntary giving which the Lord asks for isn't restricted just to income. It includes all our closely held resources—time, talents, and other treasures. Money is especially important, however, because this is usually what we hold onto the tightest. Financial tithing is the most practical way to insure a constant effort at simplifying our lives. Money gives a tangible measure of our willingness to stop clinging to our false securities and to grow in trust of the Father's care for us. Tithing is a fluid concept with few rules. Each man must prayerfully make it take shape in his own life. Therefore, I won't lay out concrete rules, but instead offer some ideas which are working for other fathers and myself.

The most practical way to approach tithing is to agree with your wife on the percentage of your income which will be given over to God's work. You must decide how much to give and where to give it. Your local parish, your diocese, the universal Church, or any ministering body is worthy to receive your contribution, but don't forget the domestic church—your home. Your home is the place where the Lord forms your family. Think of your home as a place where God's Spirit dwells and ministers through you and your family; then equip your home for the task. Some men I know have enlarged their homes to support a style of life which requires more space for

people and for worship. Don't be stingy in using your resources to support your ideals and your simplified life style!
The tithe should be a voluntary allocation of what we earn and
what we have to be distributed between the institutional
church, which serves our ecclesiastical needs, and the domestic
church which serves our practical ones.

In fact, the process of deciding how much to tithe is usually
much simpler—if not easier—than deciding where to give.
Years ago, when a family's entire life revolved around a local
parish, the source of the Church's ministry was much easier to
identify. But today the Church is a more complex institution
and we must be more discerning. Christians have many claims
on their generosity, but our tithe should support effective
ministry.

While a portion goes to our local church or parish, some of
our tithe should probably be sent to other ministering bodies,
national and international charities, or missionary organizations. Here are some guidelines to help you discern which of
these organizations deserve your support:

1. Is the organization communicating a message which is
   scriptural and consistent with church teaching?
2. Is the ministry effective? Are people responding to it?
3. Are the leaders models for what they teach?
4. Is the organization God-oriented and not self-glorifying
   or self-perpetuating?
5. Does the organization have a standard of excellence?
   Does it avoid waste?

The amount which God prescribes for the tithe may vary,
but generally we are asked to contribute at least one tenth of
our gross earned income. This may sound like a great deal, but
I'm sure many Christians are already being quite generous—
perhaps even to the level of ten percent—without even realizing it. Look up the miscellaneous charitable deductions for
your income tax. You'll find that ten percent might be well
within reach. We will also discover that ten percent is only a
minimum; all we have belongs to the Lord. The Spirit wants to
draw out even more of the ballast which weighs us down. This
pattern of giving isn't an option for us; it's part of God's plan

for our health and well-being. If you're not already tithing, try it. You will find that you are much freer with God's blessing and a maximum of ninety percent than you were on your own, with one hundred percent.

Fathers should not neglect to teach their children about tithing. When our oldest son got his first part-time job, I sat down with him to explain it. He was a little cautious and I could have prepared better, but our son understood. He decided how much to give and where to give it, then submitted his plan for my approval. A good seed was planted; now I simply review periodically how he's doing.

The younger children also need to be taught about tithing. We used the opportunity presented by a garage sale, which the kids ran, to introduce the concept to them. We asked them to give away ten percent of their earnings on the sale to a particular need in the world. They cheerfully cooperated by sending the tithe for relief of famine in Bangledesh, a pressing need at the time. They were proud of what they did and no guilt was left to steal the fruit of the Spirit.

As tithing became a way of life for me and my family, I had to be careful not to make it an idol in itself. God doesn't need our money. He desires *us*. We are not pacifying a hungry God by tithing. We give some of our resources away, so that we can also learn how to give ourselves away.

About this time you might be saying to yourself: "All this to encourage simplicity?" The answer is yes; because it isn't easy to simplify a human life. Without God, it's impossible!

CHAPTER TEN

Fidelity to Covenant:
Faith and Faithfulness

A few years ago, Anna and I attended a Marriage Encounter weekend. Although we had begun to experience spiritual renewal years before, we felt the Encounter would add a new dimension to our lives. It did. Through that weekend, I got my first insight into the third element of Christian maturity—fidelity to covenant.

We began our Encounter by telling our spouses that quality we most appreciated about them. I couldn't wait to see what Anna said about me. I expected a glowing report on my sexual prowess or some other ego-boosting quality, but Anna's notebook had only one word—"Faithfulness." Faithfulness? How dull! I was crushed, but soon I came to see that Anna was listening to the Spirit. With some time to think, I remembered the words at Mt. Carmel: Balance, Simplicity, and Fidelity to Covenant.

Fidelity to covenant means perseverance in committed love. Fidelity is not a common word today and it's also not a common virtue. This quality of being faithful grows in us as we grow in relationship with God. It stems from an initiative which God takes in our lives, and it is expressed in selfless love—the way of covenant.

A Christian father is called to reflect the fidelity of God by learning to trust in the promises of the Father and in the covenant pledge that God will be faithful.

The Fidelity of God and Man

Faith comes from the initiative of God; it is a free gift. It is the beginning of our self-surrender to Jesus. Although the gift of faith involves our total person, it is initially discovered in our minds and hearts. But when faith remains only a mental or emotional assent, it is limited.

The seed of faith is largely dormant until we act on what we believe. When faith is stirred into action, it becomes faithfulness or fidelity. This is the call of each Christian to a living, vibrant, active faith. It means hearing and obeying the Gospel, not just pondering it. It is the faith and good works which James speaks of (Jas 2:14-26).

It has never been easy to live in faith. The early Christians realized this very quickly. They proclaimed Jesus as Lord, but as the iron fist of Rome came down on them, the cost of being an active believer began to mount. Many believed, but few had the courage to die for what they believed. Then and now, faithfulness has a price. The price is death to self.

Like all virtues which strengthen a father, fidelity must begin with and flow from our relationship with God. He is always faithful. We need his holiness to sustain the call which we have received.

I have a favorite bookmark which states clearly: "My God is a Faithful God." On the reverse side are three scripture quotes from the beginning, the middle, and the end of the Bible, showing us the wonderful promises contained throughout God's word:

There hath not failed one word of all his good promise. (1 Kgs 8:56)

Forever, O Lord, thy word is settled in heaven. Thy faithfulness is unto all generations. (Ps 119:89-90)

God is faithful, by whom ye were called unto the fellowship of his Son Jesus Christ our Lord. (1 Cor 1:9)

These words were written by men who knew they were sinners and who had experienced testing and failure. Solomon,

David, and Paul knew that the source of any good in them was of God and not of themselves. The Spirit will consistently lead us back to this point. Faithfulness comes from God and he shares it with us as his gift.

God shows his fidelity in many ways, but the one which touches us most deeply is love. The Father chose to insure our security in his word by sharing his love with us. Aside from the angels, we are the only creatures who have received this gift from the Father. As we discover how to receive and share his love, we become secure in who we are as God's children.

I came to realize the faithfulness of God when I was first touched by his unconditional love on my Cursillo weekend. On that Sunday, I had no doubt that the One who had touched me would be faithful in his love forever. God's plan for each of us consists of this: that we come to know just how much we are loved by him who is love. Once we experience that truth in our lives, no one and no thing can ever dismiss it from our consciousness. When a child meets his true father, the child knows it and he clings close to his father. The "author" of our life is God.

I have become deeply aware of how faithful God is upon reflecting on how conditional my human love is. I attach many conditions to my love. Loving is easier when circumstances are right, when others are lovable and not needy, when they think like me and cause me no pain, and when they do not reflect my own sins. Yes, my love can be very conditional. Yet, he who is faithful can be trusted to love, regardless of the circumstances.

Jesus went to the cross to vividly demonstrate what ends faithful love will go to. As we stare at Calvary, yielding our fears and concerns, we can touch God's power to change our lives; he will infuse in us his heart of faithfulness. God can make us into radical lovers. "All of us, gazing on the Lord's glory with unveiled faces, are being transformed from glory to glory into his very image by the Lord who is the Spirit" (2 Cor 3:18).

On that Marriage Encounter, Anna paid me a great compliment when she said my best quality was faithfulness. With increased awareness, I have come to see how important this virtue is for all Christian fathers. A family grows in trust of a God they can't see by experiencing a staunch living faith in a man they can see.

When we accept God's love, we quickly realize our weakness and dependence on his grace. This draws us deeper into the mystery of agape love. Thus the cycle continues: We need love and God is there to love us. His love overflows in us, stirs our faith, and teaches us to trust. Our trust and hope in him brings about an active response in our wives and children, and their needs drive us back to our source of strength. In our acknowledged weakness and dependence on him, God can bless us beyond belief.

Much of the world we live in is indifferent and hostile to this cycle of faith, hope, and love. The pull of our world is mainly toward self-fulfillment, not fidelity and sacrifice. No one gives much credit to a father who lives a simple, faithful life. Commitment to anything is scorned. Common questions are: "What's in it for me?" and, "How can I get the most for the least effort?" These patterns of selfishness are found in our government, our schools, our offices, our homes, and even the Church. The world seems to offer more for less, while God is asking for our total person. A man who sets his heart on the Lord and his Kingdom will battle a constant temptation to yield to values and patterns which conflict with the truth he believes. This combat is the hub of the renewed cycle of fruitful fatherhood.

Trials and Testing

Trials and testing are two tools which God uses to bring us to maturity, but they are realities we would rather avoid. Just as exercise is painful yet productive of good physical health, so do trials and obstacles build our faithfulness.

Like an undeveloped muscle, faith must be built to its potential through constant stimulation, contraction, and relaxation. Trials and temptation are the stimuli which require an exercise of our spiritual muscles. As we encounter troubles, we usually ask God to take the pain away, but he does not always do this. When a difficult situation persists after our plea for the Shepherd's help, we can be fairly sure that God wants to use this occasion to help us grow deeper in faith.

Scripture teaches us plainly about the value of trials. "The discipline of the Lord, my son, disdain not; spurn not his reproof; for whom the Lord loves he reproves, and he chastises the son he favors" (Prv 3:11-12). James writes even more clearly: "My brothers, count it pure joy when you are involved in every sort of trial. Realize that when your faith is tested this makes for endurance. Let endurance come to its perfection so that you may be fully mature and lacking in nothing" (Jas 1:2-4). Just as we use discipline to teach our children, the Father must occasionally deal with us in stronger ways.

A good description of how God uses trials and testing can be found in Bob Mumford's book *The Purpose of Temptation*. Using scriptural examples from the Old and New Testaments, Mumford vividly describes how God grows us under trial.

As fathers experience the pain of trials and temptations, we realize that here is exactly where Jesus can help us. He meets us in our most vulnerable condition and delivers us, not just from the particular pain, but from the fear of facing it. Our most intimate relationship with the Shepherd occurs as we clutch onto his robe, slowly making our way through a minefield of temptation. When we reach the other side, we finally realize more deeply what it means to be a son of God and to have a Savior.

What in particular can trials and temptations do for us?

First, they build a deeper ability in us to serve others. When we have overcome trouble and gained a stronger faith, we are more able to encourage our weaker brothers and sisters. Our faithfulness creates a dynamic which draws out deeper faith from those who look to us for leadership.

Trials help us establish ourselves more firmly on our foundation in the Lord. "Anyone who hears my words and puts them into practice is like the wise man who built his house on rock" (Mt 7:24). Jesus is the rock, yet all of us build part of our lives on the sand of our own plans and our strength. We find out quickly how insecure our sandy foundation is when the troubled waters of temptation begin to wash over our house of faith. This experience causes us to appreciate how solid and faithful our Savior really is.

Trials and testing also teach us the true limit of our faith and humility. An occasional trip into the desert reminds us of our potential for both evil and good. These excursions do not involve a total fall. They are more of a slip or a bump. God knows when our pride begins to govern our hearts and he will use trials to teach us the true extent of our reliance on him. "Before his downfall, a man's heart is haughty, but humility goes before honors" (Prv 18:12).

Our struggle with trials and temptations can produce the good fruit of fidelity in us, but we should guard against a subtle emotional trap. This is the fear of rejection. We fear that we will not be accepted by others; that our desire to be loved will be thwarted. Fear of rejection can hold us back from acting boldly to confront and overcome the temporary pain which is part of growing in faith.

We all have experienced rejection to some degree, since none of us will be loved perfectly until we are with the Lord. A man of God must expect some rejection if he is to be a faithful follower of Jesus. However, the rejection of this world should only drive us deeper into relationship with the Father, where we will find no limitation on love or understanding.

At Calvary, Jesus faced the most complete rejection possible and he showed us how to deal with it. At the apex of rejection, caused by gathering of the sin of man onto himself, Jesus made two cries: "My God, my God, why have you forsaken me?", then, "Father into your hands I commend my Spirit" (Mt 27:46; Lk 23:46). Crushed by mankind's sin, he pushed past the rejection and gave even that to the Father. This is the key for us. When we are rejected by those who see Jesus in us, we can give these feelings of rejection to the Father. This isn't easy, but God's love is stronger than our feelings. In time and with prayer, we will heal.

One man in public life who stands as a fine example of the perseverence God wants us to have is Martin Luther King. As I learned more about Dr. King's life, I was strengthened in my faith. He moved against overwhelming odds, with only a deep faith in God and the principles of justice to stir his followers. In his speeches, he would repeat over and over, "I believe." Slowly but surely his followers' strength and conviction grew; even in the face of death, King continued to speak and act in faith. His life shows the power of faith to overcome staggering odds and the most intense rejection.

Christian fathers do not have to be beaten down by trials. We can say with Paul, "We even boast of our afflictions! We know that affliction makes for endurance and endurance for tested virtue, and tested virtue for hope. And this hope will not leave us disappointed, because the love of God has been poured out in our hearts through the Holy Spirit who has been given to us" (Rom 5:3-5).

As we consider how Jesus uses trials to help us, there is one consistent lesson. This is: Always aim to please the Father and do not seek approval from men. We must learn to seek approval only from God and not be subject to common wisdom.

Models of Faith

To grow in a virtue like faithfulness, we all need models. The Church and scripture offer an abundant supply of saints and other models of faith who can be examples to us. Let us first briefly consider two men of the Old Testament who were called to fidelity beyond that of their peers.

According to Hebrew scriptures, Noah was the son of Lamech and the tenth generation in descent from Adam. When an already old man, he and his family were singled out by God to become a faithful remnant. In the face of rejection and ridicule by his neighbors, he heard the word of the Lord and obeyed it. The faithfulness of one man and the obedience of his family provided a new start for a hopelessly lost race.

Another clear model of fidelity in Old Testament scripture is the prophet Hosea. He belonged to the northern kingdom and began his prophetic career in the seventh century before Christ. Hosea's personal life was a tragedy. His wife Gomer, who he loved with a deep devotion, proved to be a harlot who left him for her lovers. After her lovers deserted her, Gomer fell into slavery and asked Hosea to bring her back and protect her. Out of such bitter experiences, this man of faith developed his understanding of the Father's love which he later put into his writings. Hosea stands as a model of the love and mercy of God. He is also a human model for men who must face the pain of rejection—an unfaithful wife, a wayward child, an employer who has not extended his hand in friendship.

If Gomer symbolizes faithless Israel, Mary is the New Testament model of human fidelity. Mary, the mother of Jesus, understood faithfulness. She was both mother and disciple of Jesus, and the Gospels ascribe to her the key disposition of both roles—fidelity. Luke's Gospel in particular insists on Mary as our model of faithfulness. She listened to God's word and she kept it. Mary's response to the Annunciation holds the key for all of us: "I am the servant of the Lord. Let it be done to me as you say" (Lk 1:38). Her "yes" was the first Jesus received. Luke's portrait of Mary reminds us that one's place in the Church is not decided by privileged position, sex, or status. The faithful followers of Jesus, like seed on good ground, "hear the word in a spirit of openness, retain it, and bear fruit through perseverence" (Lk 8:15).

Reading lives of saints and holy people like these has fallen out of vogue in many religious circles today. Some teachers deny that the examples of people from another time and culture help our search for models, and claim that we must find current figures who are more relevant to modern life. Well, where are they? Are there modern heroes who can stir up God's gift in us and encourage a life of willing obedience to his word? Unfortunately, such heroes are in very short supply. Ask your children who their heroes are. They will probably mention Superman, Spiderman, Wonderwoman, and the Incredible Hulk—figures of pure fantasy. To these we can add sports heroes drawing million dollar salaries. Such figures are popular because, as a people, we are starving for real heroes. Like our Christmas wrappings, the super-heroes are a reflection of the shallowness of our times.

As we are turned back to God's plan, we will discover a Father who is ready, willing, and able to reveal the models we need. In short order he can begin building human fathers back into symbols of fidelity which can inspire their children.

Covenant Love

The term "covenant" is not a word we use regularly. Yet it lies at the heart of the Old Testament. Covenant is the backbone of the relationships between God and his people—the guarantee of God's faithfulness. The doctrine of covenant also underlies the action of Jesus Christ. He is the high priest of the New Covenant who sealed the covenant with his blood.

The Old Testament uses two Hebrew words to describe God's relationship with his chosen people, Israel. These words, *berith* and *hesed*, were drawn from the description of agreements among men, families, and nations. God taught his people about their relationship with him by building on concepts and words which were familiar, just as Jesus preached a gospel in terms and concepts that were familiar to men of his time.

Berith was the term for solemn agreements among men. They usually took three forms: between friends to provide legal force (1 Sm 18:3); between two rulers to fix spheres of influence or terms of peace (Gn 21:22; 1 Kgs 5:12); and between a tribe and its slaves (Jer 34:8). The Hebrew people sealed covenant in a solemn ceremony. The word berith also describes how the parties to the covenant were joined together. It comes from the same root as "fetter" or "to bind," suggesting that the covenant will bind the parties together in an unchanging, secure fashion.

Hesed meant covenant love or loyalty. A covenant established an artificial blood relationship between the parties. Like members of the same family, they were to relate to each other in the closest terms. Their relationship was to be an intimate one.

The Israelites were very familiar with covenants between humans, but when God used this term to describe the relationship he wanted with his people, it was difficult to believe.

They could only understand some aspects of the covenants offered to them. These included the original covenant between God and Abraham (Gn 15:22-26) which gave Israel possession of Canaan; the covenant between God and David (2 Sm 7) which guaranteed the perpetual monarchy in David's house; and the covenant between God and Levi (Ex 32:29; Dt 10:18) which conferred permanent priesthood on that family. However, Israel never quite grasped the extent of the intimacy God wanted to have with his people when he made the covenant at Sinai with Moses. The law and the rules for personal behavior became more important to them than *hesed*—covenant love. They missed the heart of Yahweh as he reached out with a Father's love to his rebellious children.

Let's look at what God told Moses about the relationship he wanted before he gave him the Ten Commandments and other regulations.

A few months after their encampment at Sinai, Moses went up the mountain and God spoke of his intentions and his heart's desire. "Thus shall you say to the house of Jacob; tell the Israelites: You have seen for yourselves how I treated the Egyptians and how I bore you up on eagle wings and brought you here to myself. Therefore, if you hearken to my voice and keep my covenant, you shall be my special possession, dearer to me than all other people, though all the earth is mine" (Ex 19:3-5). The people heard God say that they would be his chosen people, but the conditions of that promise fell on deaf ears. The people thought God chose them to be a privileged class, but in reality he called them to *service*. This confusion still lingers with us today.

The Old Testament clearly documents Israel's unfaithfulness to Yahweh, coupled with the Father's continuous efforts to restore the relationship. The pain God's people endured came from their stubborness and rebellion. This is a consistent pattern in our relationship with God. Throughout history man's response to God's open hand has too often been either a turned back or a clenched fist.

Catastrophe befell unfaithful Israel. About 600 years before Christ, Babylon destroyed Jerusalem and carried the people into exile. As the people were being led off into captivity,

Jeremiah remained among the ruins of Jerusalem and proclaimed the word of the Lord which we recognize today as "the gospel before the gospel." "The days are coming, says the Lord, when I will make a new covenant with the house of Israel and the house of Judah. It will not be like the covenant I made with their fathers the day I took them by the hand and led them forth from the land of Egypt; for they broke my covenant and I had to show myself their master—this is the covenant which I will make with the house of Israel after those days—I will place my law within them, and write it upon their hearts; I will be their God, and they shall be my people" (Jer 31:31-33).

The stage was now set for a final act in the Father's plan to save a hopelessly lost people. God would make a New Covenant which could not be revoked by disobedience because God himself was guaranteeing it. The Lord of the universe proclaimed himself *berith*—bound to his people. The promises of God in Jeremiah 31 are not rewards for good behavior; they are the regulations of a new relationship between God and all his children, made possible through grace—God's action, not ours. In the Old Covenant, God demanded obedience. In the New Covenant he promised that his Spirit would work directly in the hearts of men. The nature of this action was called *hesed*—covenant loyalty and faithfulness.

The New Covenant would not set the Mosaic law aside; rather it would add a new personal dimension to the fatherly relationship of God to his people. Jesus would teach us to call God "Abba." God would acknowledge his children as *family*. In the New Covenant, God took the initiative. He threw away all the options and promised unconditional love to his children, despite their proven inability to accept or be worthy of his love. Through our adoption as Gentile sons, we have become rightful heirs with the Jews to that promise.

Covenant vs. Contract

God's grace, and our acceptance of that grace at Baptism, tie us to Jesus—his Word and his Son. This is a binding agreement concluded among friends. It is very different from our modern understanding of contract, which actually sets two parties at odds with one another, in adversary positions. An example from my business career illustrates the difference well.

I worked for a speciality sub-contractor who furnished and installed complex interiors for major buildings. My employer and I were friends, but to insure faithfulness to the sensitive relationship I had with company clients, a restrictive covenant was included in my contract. My employer promised me complete access to records, files, and the full authority to represent the company in negotiations with clients in a particular area. In return, I promised not to use that privileged position to set up a competitive business. My employer and I were bound in faith to obey these rules. Even the civil courts recognize the binding nature of this kind of agreement. No monies are exchanged in a covenant, simply reciprocal faith.

In contrast to this restrictive covenant, our company signed many contracts with major construction firms, institutions, and corporations which promised specified goods and services in return for a fixed amount of money. There is little language of faith in this kind of legal document. As soon as it is signed, the parties take on an adversary relationship. The payer fights to hold onto his money as long as possible; the contractor struggles to get it away from him.

The ways of covenant love and faithfulness are contrary to the wisdom of man. Where man is protective, God is exposed. Where man wants options, God is committed. Where man wants guaranteed results, God moves unilaterally to forgive and unite. Where man is stingy with love, God's heart is boundless. We have a choice: We can retain our illusory "options," or, by faith, join fully with the Father.

The New Covenant is not just a "spiritual" binding, existing only on a theological level. We are called to live out this covenant in human relationships. Some of our expressions of covenant are marriage, vows to religious communities, church membership and solemn agreements in renewal or life-style communities. In all these relationships, we actualize our commitment to God through a promise to be faithful to others.

The marriage covenant is the form of commitment or

vocation most of us choose. We cannot deal with marriage in detail in this book, but it is true to say that entering marriage is much easier than living it. The marital covenant is the deepest of human relationships; a most effective and available vehicle for death to self. I was able to stay on the periphery of that challenge for many years, but not today. As Anna and I seriously attempt to change our style of life and our hearts, we have discovered how little we know about loving with God's heart. A man and woman experience the joy and power which the Lord wants for all committed relationships only when they constantly return to the fidelity of God.

The marriage covenant is at the heart of God's work among men. For many of us, marriage is the way we learn about faithfulness. When two are melted into one, fired in the crucible of life, others may enter that covenant. Family is formed. The Spirit accomplishes his basic work—to bring unity out of diversity. Unity, a principal quality of God, is expressed to man.

Church and Community

The joining together of families into community is again the work of God. Ultimately, this leads to a universal welding into what we call "church," a family of families. Jesus used the analogy of marriage to describe the Church. We, the Church, become the bride of Christ. The marital analogy is no mere intellectual concept. God wants us to *experience* church—our vocation as "bride"—in the practical details of daily life. The mystical Body of Christ can remain fairly mystical, but the wife and children who look to us for love and affection aren't mystical at all.

The marriage covenant is based on God's faithfulness and our commitment, not on human emotion. This is the key to appreciating any committed relationship. We put faith in God's promise, not in our emotions. Although the Marriage Encounter opens with a "focus on feelings," it states clearly that love is a *decision*. This truth is opposed by many values of our world which tend to pull us into emotional, not faithful commitments. While our emotions express how we feel, we cannot use them as criteria for how we act or who we are.

Since God's commitment through Jesus is an irrevocable promise of fidelity, our covenants with each other must reflect the same permanence. Marriage and other vowed relationships are meant for a life time. That obviously reduces our options. God has thrown out his options in reaching out to us; we are asked to reciprocate. A covenant relationship is forever! Once we make a life commitment, we can get down to the serious business of being perfected in grace and of becoming more like Jesus.

The scriptural model for both fidelity in commitment and church is the human body, an analogy which St. Paul describes in the fourth and fifth chapters of his letter to the Ephesians. Grace can be seen as blood pumping through the body to guarantee life; hierarchical structures are the frame which keeps the body erect; the individual bones as the people of God. The ligaments which hold the various members together are the *hesed*—covenant love. When Paul sought to describe faithful, selfless, everlasting love, he referred to the ligaments—the tough wrapping of tissue which connects the bones and protects their exposed ends. "Through him (Christ the head) the whole body grows, and with the proper functioning of the members joined firmly together be each supporting ligament, builds itself up in love" (Eph 4:16). It is covenant love that holds together both the universal Church and our little church, the family, under the stress of selfishness and sin.

As renewal matures in the Church, many laymen desire to extend their covenant to others in some form of shared life. This has led to vowed apostolates and covenant communities in which married, single, and religious men and women make solemn commitments to share their lives. The formation of visible unity among men is not easy. When their common ideal is Christ, we know the power comes from God's Spirit.

A community or extended family can support and challenge our growth in faith, but it cannot put into our hearts what is not already alive. For corporate life to be successful, basic relationships must be in good order. This means that our relationships with God, wife, and children must be whole and secure, if a broader common life is to be more than an escape into fantasy or an avoidance of our basic responsibilities.

Although God offers his love without reservation or condition, we can be tricked into avoiding it. As the Holy Spirit works to unite the Body of Christ, the forces of evil work to divide it. We must not allow the Adversary to steal our inheritance by deception. Our mind is the battlefield where the war of relationships is fought. In our human condition, we assume, we suspect, we fear that we will lose, we judge, we hate. Jesus nevertheless continues to offer us covenant love. We can reach out and accept that love on a spiritual and a human level. Any force within or outside of us that would fetter us to ourselves is not from God and must be resisted at all costs. *Hesed* is God's gift to those who risk and reach out.

Building Faithfulness

Two important steps to build the faithfulness which binds man to God are: (1) trusting God and (2) establishing concrete goals. The first step is an act of the will. We put our trust in God's fidelity to covenant and believe his promises. His power can't flow through us unless we stretch the limit of our expectations. This kind of radical trust in God is built on the prayer of faith, which is fully open to the will of God, taking him at his word.

Setting concrete goals further exercises our will and stirs our faith. We challenge our claims of faith with definite steps. Faithfulness grows as we define specific goals for ourselves and decide to live up to our commitments.

One thing which can block our receipt of God's grace is our own posture. Are we prepared to put his gift to use? God knows our hearts. If we aren't ready to change, he must wait. Grace is not stored in us; it flows as we are prepared to accept and use it. As we come humbly before our God, with open hands and an open heart and mind, he is free to give us all we ask for.

As we grow in trust, we should begin seeing ourselves as

living saints. The saint of today is someone who has opened his heart to God's word and is drawn to a radical response to the Gospel. A new vision of ourselves can grow, based on faith.

This style of life may lead us in a direction which is contrary to human wisdom and to the views of well-meaning friends. The path which Jesus lays out for us often demands the courage to be different and to look foolish. The call to Christian fatherhood is this kind of path. It is strewn with human and spiritual obstacles which would turn us back to safer ground, but the Spirit is calling us to persevere and to move on to a posture which looks very different from that which is familiar to the world.

Saints in the past usually acted in a way that brought them into conflict with their peers. Saints of today must be prepared to do the same. The father who has decided to fast or abstain from drinking or smoking can look absurd to business cronies on a binge. The couple with "enough" children who are moved to adoption or foster parenting may find chilliness and ridicule from their neighbors. The man who is willing to withdraw from high income endeavors to allow himself time to be a Christian father will not find great understanding when attempting to explain his call to previous colleagues. The ways of God are not those of men.

The second way we build our fidelity is to establish clear and positive patterns of response to others. Mother Theresa of Calcutta has said that a saint is someone who does little things well. We build our capacity to receive God's gift by changing the way we live our day-to-day lives. This is a hard but fruitful way to actualize faith.

Each day we have dozens of small opportunities to express faithfulness. A child observes and responds to the small signs of caring that his parents display. They especially notice the attitude with which care is shown. These are the opportunities for earning our crown and running the race. They're not terribly glamorous but they build up the faith in us. Faithfulness is a pattern of behavior, and like any pattern it is initiated in our attitudes.

I try to do this by identifying and changing my negative patterns of response. For example, laziness still lingers in me. When Anna or the children ask me for something which requires some effort on my part, that weakness wants to say "no." I've caught this "no" response enough to see that it is an ingrained pattern. To change this I've decided to respond positively to any request which was not selfish and which was within my power to grant. When in doubt, I ask for time to pray about it. Eventually this new pattern will replace the old one. When a positive response becomes my normal one, I can bear down on another pattern that should change.

Replacing negative patterns is one of the ways the Spirit moves to perfect us in grace. The new pattern which God wants requires a decision and commitment to stick to that decision. This engages the will and opens the door to further decisions for the Lord.

Fidelity is expressed in action, not in words or good intentions. We can think about all the things we "should have done" or "will do someday," but what counts is what we do today. Thoughts about the past can discourage us, and needless speculations about the future can confuse or bring fear into us. But Jesus is the Lord of all time, especially today. He taught us to pray for our "daily bread." It is in working with the grace of the present moment that we fully cooperate with the Spirit. Grace, the indwelling of God, is alive today. It can't be frozen and stored for the future.

The external evidence of fidelity—our behavior patterns—are motivated by our attitudes. The key attitude which produces fidelity is an active sense about life, and especially about God. We are called to be men of action, not observers of the passing scene. A holy zeal should permeate all of what we do, think, and say. Even our listening can be active, expecting to hear God instructing us, telling us about our next step in faith.

Active listening means being ready to respond to those first impulses of the Spirit, those we sense before our logical Western minds have a chance to analyze what is happening. How many times have you ignored those gentle first impulses in situations, only to discover later that it was God speaking. Timidity can cause us to be afraid of looking foolish or making mistakes. The Spirit, however, can easily re-direct an active response which may be off-target, but it is hard to move a passive man who just sits and says "I should." A growing charism of fidelity will begin to eliminate the word "should" from our thoughts about ourselves.

One more step in actualizing our faith is the constant need for clarity in our human and spiritual relationships. God has been clear with us in the revelation of his will for man in the scriptures. We should be clear with each other. "Do two walk together unless they have agreed" (Am 3:3)?

Thus, as we expect more of those who walk with us in faith, it is beneficial to make clear agreements which define how we will live out our part in God's covenant. We do this when we enter into marriage. The liturgy and the scriptures relate, in the presence of the partners and to the community which witnesses the covenant, just what each partner intends to do.

I am discovering that this approach can be extended to the family and beyond. We are now working on a family covenant which will be a tool to remind us what we are professing and how we intend to live that out. Christian communities are also clarifying their agreements with written covenants. These documents make our faith real; they add power to our words and they help us to avoid confusion and discouragement.

The theme of fidelity is one which needs reinforcement for modern man. Pope Paul VI spoke these words in February 1966 to the couples and families of the world, "It is as true today, as in the past and always, children find in the life of their parents the most profound formation of fidelity to God, while the parents find in obedience to God the certainty of the grace they need for their task as Christian educators."

Families will look to faithful parents, and especially fathers, to learn that God is always faithful to his covenant of love.

Part Four

Leading Your Family

CHAPTER ELEVEN

Loving Authority: Headship

Several years ago I made an interesting discovery about myself. Having been involved in renewal activities for a while, I was content with my progress in the Christian life. Nevertheless, there seemed to be a growing restlessness in me. As time went on, I realized the Lord was stirring a deeper hunger for change.

One evening I told a priest that things were going pretty well for me. The priest smiled and asked, "What then, do you want of God?" My immediate response sounded foreign to my ears: "I want to become a real lover." The reply came from God's Spirit within me. I realized it was an honest answer to a honest question. But what is a "real lover"?

To understand the nature of love, we must go to its source— God, the only real lover. God is love! He is all perfect, full of mercy and kindness. But God has revealed that his nature has a particular quality to it: it contains authority. "There is no authority except from God, and all authority that exists is established by God" (Rom 13:1).

To understand how love and authority exist within and because of God, we must look to the Trinity. God has revealed himself as a community of persons living in intimate relationship. Although our grasp of the trinitarian mystery is limited, we can see the loving relationships in the Trinity as a model for our human families. A peaceful and harmonious home can exist only when a selfless, serving, caring authority is being exercised.

Without godly authority, a home can easily become a place of competition and individualism. With the heavenly family as a model, we see that oneness is the fruit of loving authority.

Man also needs authority if his social structures are to function properly. Aristotle stated this centuries ago: "He who is unable to live in society, or who has no need because he is sufficient for himself, must be either a beast or a god." In short, because society is natural to man, whether it be the society of the family or of the state, authority is necessary.

Despite our need, we tend to fear and mistrust authority. This might stem from past experiences with unjust authority, or a misunderstanding of its true meaning. Just as true love is not manipulation, spiritual authority is not authoritarianism. Rather, our authority enables us to serve others so that they may experience God's love. To grow in these areas, we must be willing to allow the Holy Spirit to change our old ways of thinking and behaving about authority. In short, the price is the renewal of our mind. "Do not conform yourselves to this age but be transformed by the renewal of your mind, so that you may judge what is God's will, what is good, pleasing and perfect" (Rom 12:2).

Authority is a controversial topic which I would like to avoid if I could. However, there is no other way to communicate the full nature of God's love. The loving authority of God is indispensible to spiritual leadership in a Christian home. Headship and submission are its "cutting edges," the processes through which authority is exercised. The essence of Christian fatherhood lies in accepting the authorization to exercise trinity love as head of the home.

What is Headship?

Headship is a gift from God, a way to communicate his love to a Christian family. It is a principal charism of fatherhood and an essential part of a man's role as spiritual leader in his home. It is a primary way for him to serve the Lord and his family. Headship is loving authority in action; it is our way of imitating Christ.

Both the power to love and the authority to serve have their source in God the Father. They are shared with us through Christ who is the head of the Church. The loving authority of fatherhood passes into our family through our willful submission to Christ and his Church.

The first time I heard the word "headship" was at H.O.P.E., a house of prayer in Convent Station, New Jersey. The few days which I spent with Father Jim Ferry, Bob Gallic, and the Christian community at H.O.P.E. changed my attitudes about authority and pointed me toward a whole new approach to being father of my family.

I was not prepared for the idea of fruitful and effective spiritual authority. The notion of "headship" conjured up negative reactions in my mind, but I could not ignore its visible fruit. I saw happy children, peaceful women, and humble men. My attitudes about headship did not change overnight, but a seed was planted on that visit. It didn't blossom for about a year.

For the next year, I struggled with my inability to exercise God's authority over my family. My wife and children definitely were not experiencing the fruits of effective headship. I finally realized that my problem was twofold: ignorance and lack of desire. I simply didn't know enough about spiritual authority to be effective with my family, and my ignorance allowed me to stubbornly cling to my old suspicion of the whole idea.

A year after the trip to H.O.P.E., I travelled to another community—The Word of God in Ann Arbor, Michigan. Gary and Barbara Morgan, close friends of ours, had moved to Ann Arbor from Philadelphia a few years earlier, and I knew their lives had changed for the better. Gary said a key to the change was his growth as a father. He spent hours with me explaining headship and how it serves a family. The light of God's truth broke through when he said, "Bob, headship is necessary to be sure that everyone gets loved enough." Simply put, headship is a father's way of loving his family. Without realizing it, I had been fighting something that is as natural to life as eating and sleeping. My mind was opened and conviction in my heart began.

Change came slowly. I went home to Philadelphia and tried to act like a Christian leader at home, but the results were meager. Although assenting mentally to becoming head of my home, I still resisted the idea in my will. I didn't *want* additional responsibilities. Despite my fear, the Spirit continued to draw out faith. I finally asked God to give me a desire to be willing to embrace the authority he had given me. He answered my prayer, gently opening my heart to become the man he had called me to be. As my heart opened to the Lord's love and direction, the initial seed planted at H.O.P.E. was fed and nurtured. Once my will was released, the Spirit was able to begin teaching me what I needed to know.

What I learned was a new way of looking at God and what he has taught us. Jesus revealed God's nature as *family*. Within the heavenly family, there has always existed fatherhood, unity, and authority. God the Father preserves the unity within the Trinity. A chain of authority begins with the Father and is communicated through the Spirit into the Body of Christ here on earth. This pattern of authority connecting God to his people relies on headship. Paul told the church in Corinth, "I want you to know that the head of every man is Christ; the head of a woman is her husband; and the head of Christ is the Father" (1 Cor 11:3).

Christ's headship comes from the Father. While he walked the earth, Jesus made it very clear that he acted only by authority of the Father. He didn't act on his own account, but submitted himself totally to his "Abba." For example, when challenged about his authority to cure on the Sabbath, he replied, "I solemnly assure you, the Son cannot do anything by himself—he can only do what he sees the Father doing" (Jn 5:19).

Jesus repeats over and over the necessity for headship and submission to insure unity and peace. Jesus handed on the loving authority which was rightly his to his Church, in order that his followers could be cared for. The Body of Christ is made up of human beings in human families which are called upon to share in the headship of Christ and bring the fruits of unity to a world ravaged and fragmented by sin.

Headship is a part of God's nature. It is not something invented by the Church to suggest male dominance. Neither does headship and submission imply inferiority or superiority. Jesus has explained that he is fully equal to the Father, while at the same time fully under the Father's authority. The same is true of headship in his body.

God has chosen to have men and women participate in this chain of authority in a particular way. He has established complementary and unique roles which allow us to become effective as parents and to experience the fruit of union with God. In earthly families, as in heaven, there can be no unity without clarity and submission to rightful authority. The apostle Paul describes this relationship in Ephesians: "Husbands love your wives, as Christ loved the church." "Wives should be submissive to their husbands as if to the Lord because the husband is head of his wife just as Christ is head of his body the church, as well as its savior" (Eph 5:25, 22-23).

You will notice that I reversed the order of these sentences as they appear in Ephesians. I've done this to emphasize the fact that the first hurdle to surmount in achieving God's order in the family is for the husband to unconditionally love his wife. This is the key which unlocks peace in the home. When a man begins to love his wife in a selfless way, she will submit to his authority with joy. But a man is only fooling himself if he tries to force her submission before submitting to Christ himself and treating her with respect and love.

When headship operates properly in a family, it becomes the process by which God communicates his loving authority. Christ acts as the head of the man, who in turn loves and protects his wife. Together the husband and wife exhibit a godly unity which allows the children to be directed and formed by the Holy Spirit. God's direction, communicated in this way, is as life-giving as the air we breathe. As each member of the family accepts his role in the order which Christ has established, the family experiences the blessings which the Father has ordained and planned for it.

The earlier analogy of a car's transmission, helps me to understand my role as head of my family. The gears in a transmission are parts of a linkage which work together to deliver power to the wheels, which drive the car. Similarly, a father is a link in the transmission of God's authority. Christ, the head of all families, communicates that authority to fathers, who pass it on to their wives and children. Receiving the Lord's teaching through an obedient husband and father, a family can pass it on to others. God has the power; we are his instruments; love lubricates the process.

A man can exercise headship according to the Lord's plan only by grace. The Spirit alone overcomes our human resistance to headship and permits us to live together in peace and harmony. Indeed, outside of the flow of grace, authority becomes a threat, as shown by the number of divorces, runaway children, and disintegrating families. The sad state of modern society shows that we tend to be an authority unto ourselves, rather than loving servants of God.

In God's grace, headship becomes the opposite of the "macho" vehicle it often appears to be. The man is not exalted, but is a servant, as Christ is a servant to his Church. The woman is not dominated, but rather is freed. The children do not resist authority, but realize how much they need it. God's ways are not man's; his truth is often the reverse of what human vision perceives.

This order for a family provides specific roles in the experience of loving authority, yet insures that each individual is equal before God. This is another paradox witnessed to by Jesus, who confounds human thinking. How can persons be equal, yet submissive to each other? Only God knows the answer and the indwelling of his Spirit enables it to be lived out. These statements of Jesus confirm the equality of persons in the midst of authority: "Whoever has seen me has seen the Father" (Jn 14:9); "The Father and I are one" (Jn 10:30); "The Father is greater than I" (Jn 14:28).

The headship which Christ ordains for a father is not optional; it is essential to insure the smooth transfer of God's love to each member of the family. If we refuse to accept our place, the linkage is incomplete and those we are responsible for are denied our loving protection which God planned for them. Unfortunately, the climate of our times is one of alienated individualism and hostility to authority. We are part of an age seeking a false liberation. This general rebelliousness especially saps the strength of fathers. In other times, social organizations, institutions, and other families reinforced the natural parental authority. Fathers could expect support for their values. The evil present in the world was more clearly separated from the protected environment of our homes. As a child, I knew if my father failed to notice my wrong behavior, it was bound to be corrected by another father on our block. I couldn't get too far out of line. Today, however, institutions and neighborhoods are much different. The values of secular humanism and other current philosophies are penetrating Christian homes. Unless fathers become spiritual heads, Christian families are in jeopardy.

Spiritual Authority

When a man is obedient to God and accepts his place in the line of spiritual authority, he has the right to exercise headship. This is God's provision for him and his family. The point is well illustrated in the healing of the centurion's servant (Lk 7:1-10).

This story teaches about Jesus' authority. The centurion, a military man who understands power, says to Jesus, "Just give the order and my servant will be cured. I too am a man who knows the meaning of an order, having soldiers under my command" (Lk 7:7-8).

The centurion had this right because he was under Caesar's authority. As long as he fulfilled the demands of his position, the power of Caesar was at his disposal. This is why he was able to understand Jesus' claim as Son of God. He knew that Jesus' words brought the power of God with them when he spoke. Jesus was under God's authority, and his submission to the Father allowed him to exercise that power.

A father is in the same position. If we are obedient sons, we have God's authority. God has given fathers this gift, yet we must decide whether we will exercise it or merely admire it. Unfortunately for many men, headship is like a precious but unwrapped gift. It has gone unnoticed or forgotten. Our gift can only be put to use if we decide to unwrap and use it.

The authority which God offers to a father is best described as one of personal integrity. It is not something which he gets, but rather it's what he already has by virtue of how he lives and what he's experienced. The spiritual authority fathers exercise comes from the wisdom of having faced and overcome a particular situation, through the power of Christ. It's this kind of "refining by fire" which gives strength to our words.

Although you may not like his style, General George Patton was a man who understood authority. He knew how to get results. Patton once said that an army is like a rope; you can pull it, but you can't push it. I was trained as a combat engineer officer and I know what Patton meant. When the chips are down, you have to lead people by the example you set, not by your words. When a leader wants men to move out, he can't say "you go"—he says "let's go." He gets up front and *pulls* those he's responsible for.

The role of a Christian father is one of leadership by example. He strives to protect and nurture the hearts and minds of those whom God has placed in his care. In exercising this type of authority, a man can only teach and enforce what he is living himself. There are few ribbons and medals for the father who resists evil and brings his family the leadership they need. His rewards are the joy of seeing his loved ones grow in the Lord and the inner peace which comes from hearing and obeying the command to love.

The hidden strength of a man of spiritual authority is the genuine *humility* he displays before God and his family. He does not have to shout or beat his fist to bring power to his words. The power is already there. Of course the ultimate example of a man who exercised spiritual authority while living true humility is Jesus Christ. The men of his time understood the difference: "The reason was that he taught with authority and not like their scribes" (Mt 7:29). Their religious leaders sought control through position and title; Jesus commanded authority through humble obedience to God. Jesus shows fathers that only the obedient will exercise authority in his Kingdom. He took that principle all the way to the cross.

In his book *Spiritual Authority*, Watchman Nee brings this point home. David, he writes, was subject to God's authority and made no attempt to establish his own. "Anyone who represents authority should be low and humble before God and before his people. David was truly a king set up by God, for he had the authority of God.... Then it is not so surprising that David, king though he was, was not at all conscious of his kingship, only conscious of his unworthiness. One who represents God's authority must have this blessed foolishness in him: to have authority yet to be unconscious of being an authority."

A father being used as an instrument of God's authority must have this kind of spirit: submissive to Christ and humble before the Father. If he is rebellious, that rebellion will become contagious. Only a man who is obedient to the Spirit can exercise God's authority with love.

Since spiritual authority is a gift from God, we should expect to be able to grow in this gift as we use it. Just as many Christians have discovered that charismatic gifts grow more effective as we use them, so too can we expect to grow in headship.

Authority and love come to us from the Father. We grow in both as we accept more of God's love and grow in relationship with him. In the age of print and information, we can try to acquire this growth through knowledge alone. We can read books, hear tapes, and listen to gifted teachers. This will help, but only God himself can transfer his loving authority into a man's heart.

Abuses of Authority

The greatest abuse of authority is to confuse our role with that of Jesus. We are not Lord of our home. Jesus is! Neither are we the savior for our wife and children. Jesus is! A friend of mine once told me a story that illustrates this truth. His wife observed him trying to exercise authority at home in a heavy-handed way. One day she stopped him with the comment, "We have one Lord in this house and that's enough!" Headship means that we are called to *imitate* Jesus and reflect the Father's love to our family; we're not called to replace God. Spiritual authority can tempt a man's pride. It has power. We are to use God's authority, not abuse it.

The most common abuses of a father's authority are anger, harshness, and negative speech. I continue to struggle against these tendencies in myself and have seen the harm they can do to a family.

Anger seems to be a common problem with many men. Sometimes, it goes way back to experiences in our childhood when parents unknowingly vented their anger on us. We can absorb this habit and occasionally do the same thing to our own family.

Anger in itself is neither good nor bad. It is usually a reaction, often justified, against something that does need correction and change. If we react maturely, the anger leads to change and our emotion is defused. But often situations don't change, and our anger can become a real problem. If we try to repress this emotion, it will only build up and cause a worse explosion later. If we direct anger toward other people, we can do grave harm. So what do we do with it?

The answer is to give our anger to Jesus and refuse to act wrongly because we are emotionally distressed. Jesus can get us through an emergency and later, when the temperature is lower, he will usually point out the true source of our anger and show us how to change. Our relationship with Jesus is the only one which can handle this volatile emotion without damage. For our part, we need to resist the common idea today that destructive emotions must be expressed and acted upon. With God's help we *can* control our emotions; they do not have to control us.

Frustration is often caused by failure to handle the early warning signs of anger properly. All of us, especially fathers, tend to vent that frustration on those who love us the most— our families. Often it helps to discuss frustration with those close to us, but it can hurt to express it thoughtlessly. Paul warns us in clear terms, "Fathers, do not anger your children" (Eph 6:4).

Harshness is the way an angry man deals with the people around him. It is contagious and will be picked up, especially by young children. When we deal with children harshly about something important, they absorb our anger and usually ignore the point which we were trying to make.

The third abuse of spiritual authority which manifests itself in many men is a pattern of negative thinking and a resultant habit of negative speech. Negative speech is contrary to the positive nature of the Holy Spirit, and it can quickly poison the atmosphere of a family. Gossip, negative humor, and unjust criticism are prime examples.

God wants us to begin to see ourselves and others through his eyes, not by human standards. By the tone of our speech, those around us develop their self-image and their ways of behaving. We can choose to build them up by speaking "words of life" or tear them down with negative comments. Jim Katona, an old friend, once taught me, "There's a sleeping Jesus in every person we meet. We must simply wake him up." That is done through encouragement and affirmation.

Abuses of our authority temporarily blur the image of God for our family, but Jesus doesn't want it to remain that way. Our sin doesn't destroy the process of conversion to Jesus; it only retards it. Through repentance, we can claim the blood of Christ and the redeeming power of grace. This is what it means to have a savior! God has provided the means for us to persevere and experience freedom from our sin.

The potential for divine love exists in an earthly family. As fathers, we can choose to exercise our authority in a fashion which makes the ways of God attractive and believable. We are called to be a healing, positive presence in our homes. Our tongues, with their enormous potential for either blessing or curses, can be harnessed for the Kingdom. We can experience the peace, love, and joy which God intended for us as we continue to turn our minds and hearts over to Jesus for healing and restoration.

We have come to see headship as a gift through which a Christian father communicates the loving authority of God to his family. The key to spiritual leadership in any Christian environment is found in the willingness of the person having rightful authority to accept and use it properly.

My close friend, Father Dan Cavanaugh, has a favorite theory which tells us how well our headship is working. Father Dan says, "People go where they are loved the most." If your family is happy to be with you at home, your headship is working.

CHAPTER TWELVE

Submission:
Becoming Useful for God

At the turn of the century, a slight man, living in a Trappist monastery in Syria, wrote these words:

> Father, I abandon myself into your hands; do with me what you will, whatever you may do, I thank you; I am ready for all, I accept all.
>
> Let only your will be done in me, and in all your creatures—I wish no more than this, O Lord. Into your hands I commend my life; I offer it to you with all the love of my heart.
>
> For I love you, Lord, and so need to give myself, to surrender myself into your hands, without reserve, and with boundless confidence.
>
> For you are my Father.

This prayer, known as "The Prayer of Abandonment," was written by Charles de Foucauld, later known as Brother Charles of Jesus. Born in the later 1800s in a devout Catholic family, he lost his faith in his teens, became a lazy drunkard, and was almost expelled from the French army. He was converted by a sermon on Matthew's Gospel which said that Jesus always took the last place for himself and that no one has yet been able to take that place from him. Jesus' total abandonment to his Father's will penetrated Charles' mind and changed his life. He eventually went to the Sahara Desert and submitted himself totally to Christ and a life of prayer. He modeled his spirituality on the simple life which Jesus led in Nazareth,. seeing that the Messiah was formed, not in power, but in humble submission to his Father in Heaven and to the human authority of Joseph and Mary. Charles de Foucauld's quiet witness in the African sand continues to inspire men toward surrender to God.

Submission to Christ is the abandonment of a man's will to God. The biggest obstacle to submission is pride—the root sin of our earthly father Adam. Spiritual growth cannot bypass pride, the backbone of man's rebellion. God must eventually deal with our pride if we are to become useful leaders for our families and others in the Kingdom.

We cannot exercise the Father's authority in love until we submit to him. We must allow him to break our pride and bend our will so that we may become effective spiritual leaders. Let me give you a personal example.

A Time of Breaking

After a period of learning and encouragement, I knew a lot about headship, but applying it was another matter. There still was continuing disorder in my life and in our home. I was a man who possessed knowledge about shepherding, but did not have the heart of a shepherd. I still had not decided to bend low before the Father and surrender my will. There is a big difference between knowing and doing. My knowledge of spiritual leadership acted like an anesthetic, numbing my conscience. I was becoming comfortable with a lack of fruit in spite of my awareness.

God used my wife Anna to motivate me. Anna had been patiently waiting and praying for me. One day I grumbled to her, "What do you want of me anyway?" She exploded, grabbed a pen and paper, and returned with a letter that stunned me. It was time to put my knowledge into action. Here is some of that letter:

My idea of a husband and father is a man who is on top of

his circumstances, leading the way, caring and interested in me and his children, under God. He should be defining our goals, discerning our direction, asserting himself, seeing areas of need and doing something about them in clear definitive ways. He should always be concerned about his relationship with God, our relationship, and that with his children. He should know who he is, moving ahead, not withdrawing. A positive, assertive servant, who our children could look up to and who could make a wife feel secure, protected and cared for.

The letter went on for three pages detailing how I had spent too many years with my eyes fixed on the wrong priorities. She explained how my lack of submission to God's will, and the accompanying unwillingness to exercise my spiritual authority, had caused confusion in her role: She was trying to be both father and mother.

Anna challenged me to, "Make a decision in your heart to be the kind of husband and father God wants you to be. Learn about it and live it. If you make mistakes and backslide, don't give up, but repent and go on. Make your goal a desire to live out the truth of your call to Christian manhood."

Anna's letter was written as a result of justifiable anger. It was just what I needed to get my adrenalin flowing and make a change. My pride was broken as I came to realize the shocking truth: *I* was the problem in our home! My basic rebellion to God had prevented the grace of spiritual authority from flowing into my family.

Each marriage and family has its unique features, but I believe the resistance of men in submitting to God and accepting the call to spiritual leadership is the principal problem in American society today. We can try to blame our wives, our kids, our childhood, or the Church, but God might well say, "I have given you the grace to be a father. What have you done with it?" After seeing enough men struggle with the grace of fatherhood and resist surrendering to the Lord, I believe I know where our problems lie. Fathers, there are no problems greater than those in ourselves.

In correcting the Corinthians' conduct in public worship, Paul placed the responsibility of submission squarely on the man. He instructed women of that day to wear a headcovering to visibly demonstrate submission to their husbands. Then he said to men, "A man, on the other hand, ought not to cover his head, because he is the image of God and the reflection of his glory. Woman in turn is the reflection of man's glory" (1 Cor 11:7). Although today's habits of dress have changed, the underlying principle of the scripture still applies. To fully receive God's glory and reflect it to our wives, we must take the posture of Jesus—subordinated to the Father and a servant to our families. When our wives are not radiant with peace, joy, and love, it is often our own image which we are reflecting, not the image of God which is temporarily blurred in us.

Submission

What is submission? Scripture and the experience of Christians provide some definitions.

Although submission to Christ involves external behavior, it is mostly an inner attitude of being a child. Submission is the knowledge that we are children in God's family. When we are submitted to Christ, we can admit our human weakness and confess our limitations, asking Christ (the head), and our brothers and sisters (the other members), to exercise some control over our human nature which tends toward sin.

Submission is the yielding of our hopes, our dreams, our plans, and our mistakes to others in God's kingdom. The attitude of submission opens our heart to the daily call to "repent and believe the Good News." With this attitude comes a desire to love and accept our brothers and sisters in Christ.

Our first act of submission must always be to God. Only he can teach us how to love and serve others. When a man submits totally to Christ, he is freed of the burden of himself. With that burden laid at God's feet, he can become the man God wants him to be—not the man he wants to create for himself.

In short, submission in the kingdom of God is the opposite of what "submission" means in common usage. In the secular world, the term suggests repression and captivity. But subordination to Christ enables us to achieve freedom and fulfillment. God is for us! What's more, fathers who have yielded to Christ receive power from him and the authority to exercise it. A humble man is empowered to act with God's authority, always mindful of the source of his strength.

When Jesus commissioned seventy-two new followers and sent them out to preach the good news, he said, "Be on your way, and remember: I am sending you as lambs in the midst of wolves" (Lk 10:3). The wolves were the religious authorities in the house of Israel who had already lost their spiritual power. But Jesus went on to assure his disciples that they acted for him, with ultimate power. "He who hears you, hears me. He who rejects you, rejects me. And he who rejects me, rejects him who sent me" (Lk 10:16). The power of God is with those he calls and sends forth.

Jesus has also commissioned and dispatched us—to our homes, our jobs, and our communities. Our commission is to, "Say to 'them, the reign of God is at hand'" (Lk 10:9). We do this by the example of our life. He has called us to spiritual leadership and fully equipped us for the task. The only requirement is that we submit to God as the source of our authority and love. On our own, there is little of lasting substance which we can achieve, but under God, there is no force on earth which can stop us.

Human Authority

Submission is empowered—made possible—by the Holy Spirit. The Spirit leads us into a family style of life. The Body of Christ is both a spiritual and a human reality. Yet it is human authority which provides the real test of our attitude of submission. The spiritual nature of the Body of Christ makes great theology but it is the human component which forces us to bend and learn to surrender.

The types of authority which we normally experience are ecclesiastical, civil, and functional. In all three forms, God empowers weak men to serve other weak men.

Church officials are often severely criticized for their exercise of ecclesiastical authority, but in fact the restrictions they place on our personal freedom are very slight. The ultimate standard for our actions is personal conscience; very few Church statements are rendered "infallible." Much of the criticism of Church officials happens simply because no authority can please every group in the Church. The fact that such diversity exists is a sign of the action of the Spirit. God wants unity in him, not uniformity among men.

However, the teaching authority of the Church does influence our life in a family. Until recently, this influence has been limited to moral theology rather than an affirmative pastoral direction. This emphasis is now being expanded as the Catholic bishops seek to encourage a grass roots response to their vision for family ministry. (For details, see Plan of Pastoral Action for Family Ministry, 1978, U.S. Catholic Conference.) The authority the bishops exert in this effort is a fatherly encouragement to discover and use spiritual gifts in our families and in "like-to-like" ministry within the local church setting. The pastoral authority of the Church is encouraging initiative in the laity. The rest is up to us.

Most of the restrictive authority we experience comes through civil government and the flood of codes, laws, and agencies which affect our daily lives. The enormity of bureaucratic influence on us can be easily seen as we watch a new President take office. The exuberance of campaign promises quickly fades as the man with ultimate civil authority must wrestle with the Washington bureaucracy and eventually acknowledge that his personal effect is minimal, except in times of national emergency.

Civil authority has an enormous effect on the externals of our lives, yet we are scripturally directed to respect it unless it is clearly unrighteous. Jesus acknowledged the rights of Jewish religious authorities and the Roman civil authorities, but he taught that their power had its origin in God. Civil authority has its rights until Jesus returns in glory to bring all authority back to its source—the Father.

Personal Guidance

Although they carry great power, Church and civil authority do not provide the believer with the personal direction he needs to grow in submission to Christ. These authorities are essentially impersonal, providing broad guidelines, but rarely personal direction.

Thus we need personal pastoral care, functional authority which we submit to voluntarily so we can grow in our relationship with Jesus and in our vocation of fatherhood. It can be quite difficult to voluntarily open our lives to the scrutiny of a person or a group. We come face to face with our stiff necks and a basic rebellion when we are asked to give up the last remnant of illusory personal freedom to which we all cling. Living under impersonal institutional authority is very safe. The consequences are very different, however, when we allow others to look closer at various areas of our life.

God's plan of salvation for his people consists of more than a map. He also gave us guides—Jesus, the Spirit, and each other. We have to become guides for each other in whatever areas we can. Today many fathers, aware of the need for good spiritual guidance, are voluntarily seeking it out. It is not mandatory that we have spiritual direction, but practical experience has shown me that we can only grow so far without it.

St. Teresa of Avila offered some wisdom to those in search of spiritual assistance. She suggested that we look for a prudent, rather than just a holy man. I would like to give some additional suggestions about finding the right person to give spiritual help to fathers.

The first prerequisite of your spiritual guide is that he be a friend. In our pursuit of spiritual perfection we can gloss over this obvious fact. The Cursillo offers a good slogan for the priorities in a guidance relationship: Make a friend, be a friend, lead your friend to Christ. Your guide's attitude must be first as an equal and a friend.

Consider the wisdom of Sirach 37:

A true friend will fight with you against the foe, against your enemies he will be your shield bearer... Every counse-

lor points out a way, but some counsel ways of their own...
Seek no advice from one who regards you with hostility;
from those who envy you, keep your intentions hidden...
Instead, associate with a religious man, who you are sure
keeps the commandments; who is like-minded with yourself
and will feel for you if you fall. (Sir 37:5, 7, 10, 12)

The ancient writers suggest faithfulness as the key virtue to
discern in selecting friends and spiritual counselors. We will
meet many gifted and impressive individuals as we grow in the
Lord, but a tried and true friend is our richest treasure.

The person who helps you spiritually should be more mature
in grace than yourself. The evidence of this person's maturity
should be visible, not hidden behind rhetoric. Finding someone who exemplifies the ideals of Christ will not be easy, but if
you pray and continue to seek, God will direct you to the right
person. If you can't find anyone who is significantly more mature than yourself, a person who is approximately at your level
of spirituality can certainly be helpful.

A spiritual guide must be located within a reasonable distance of where you live. He should be able to be a part of the
normal course of events in your life. Practical difficulties and
physical limitations should usually rule out having a spiritual
guide in another city. I have known men who have done this,
but these long-distance relationships often become artificial
and lack the intimacy which is essential for growth. The grass
always looks greener on the other side of the Kingdom, yet
most times we should simply accept those available to us and
expect God to provide more if we need it.

The person you ask to help you grow spiritually should be
willing to fill that role. An effective guide must have a heart of
love for you and a strong desire to see you grow to your maximum potential. He should realize that, at some point, your
continued growth may eventually demand change of guides.
Therefore, he must have an unselfish motivation for serving
you. We should avoid becoming someone else's "project." To
guard against this, begin searching for guidance among those
who have already demonstrated a capacity for unconditional

love. Beware of possessiveness or a self-serving attitude in the person you are considering to give guidance and direction.

Another characteristic to look for in a prudent confidant is the ability to spend enough time with you. Many gifted people are too busy to provide the wisdom and counsel we need. Being able is just as important as being willing. We may not discover this problem until we've met with someone a few times and noticed an impatience in him, signaled by continual glances at his watch. The person who assists you spiritually should consider you the most important person in his life at that time. His attention should be focused on you and not beyond to the next meeting or appointment.

Many readers will be wondering whether they should seek guidance from an ordained clergyman or a layman. I believe the answer is: Look to the man's gifts, and your needs, not his collar.

If your needs demand a heavy emphasis on repentance from sin or broken Church relationships, a priest who is gifted in healing and has sacramental faculties should be able to help. If your need is more oriented toward growth in your vocation as husband and father, the best choice would probably be a layman with security and confidence in his fatherhood. Some men might seek direction from both a priest and a layman. The key here is to discover your deepest need and to address that first, in the most practical way.

We should be able to separate our needs into sacramental, counseling, and vocational categories and get the best help possible to meet a specific situation. For instance, I may have a fruitful relationship with a holy priest, but wouldn't expect him to give me practical advice in an area outside his limits of experience and knowledge. For a legal problem, I'd go to a lawyer and not expect my clergyman to have all the answers.

Your spiritual guide should be open to others for wisdom when he does not have it. No one person can provide us with all the direction we need. At the same time, there is danger in having too many advisors and not actually being submitted to any of them. This can be an effective tactic to avoid confronting tough decisions and making personal changes. We should select one person to whom we will look for principal guidance, and put heavy weight on his advice. Yet expect that person to freely invite outside wisdom into our life when that is needed.

In this discussion of finding a spiritual guide, I have assumed that you are not already in a Christian community where this decision is made along with someone who has established pastoral authority. Few Christian fathers have this advantage. Most are in the position of making a personal and purely voluntary choice for spiritual guidance.

Many men who are not connected to communities mistakenly think they cannot experience the fruit of submission. That is simply not true. All men can grow in submission. If a man is part of a community where guidance relationships already exist, his path to submission will be easier. But if that is not the case, he can take the personal initiative to find the right "covering" for himself. This is possible in or out of a Christian community. All fathers should be in submission to Christ and to some delegate of Christ's authority in the local body.

At the same time, fathers should observe these cautions:

1. *Don't let the guidance relationship become an idol.*
Jesus is your shepherd. The person who acts in his place must help you to avoid becoming a worshipper of man. This can easily happen, especially when your guide is an attractive person with a multitude of gifts. No relationship should occupy more time, energy, or attention than our relationships with God and our family.

2. *You must grow to maturity and not become dependent.*
The goal of any human shepherd is to bring those under his care to maturity in Christ. Talk with your guide if this is not happening. A parent faces the same problem in helping a teenage child begin to step out of the nest. Too much freedom will cause a crash; and too little will never allow their wings to grow.

3. *Don't procrastinate out of fear of making mistakes.*
Sometimes we become so cautious in attempting to gather the best spiritual wisdom that we miss God's timing. We

shouldn't procrastinate on decisions, but go ahead in confidence that God will correct us if we are not on the right track. The old army slogan applies here: "Some decision is better than none at all." Once we're in motion, God can correct us. He can work very well in situations which appear to be failures. There are very few decisions which can't be modified or corrected to better line up with the Lord's perfect plan.

Discernment

When all is said and done, the assistance we receive from another person is just that—assistance. We must make our own decisions and stand personally responsible for our actions. The Church teaches very clearly that, in the end, it is our personal conscience which must be at peace with our decisions.

This process is called discernment; it simply means taking the best wisdom you can gather, then thinking and deciding for yourself. Submission does not free you from being accountable for your decisions; it only provides outside discernment to help you in the process of thinking and decision-making.

Sometimes we need to take advice from a select group of people before making important decisions. If so, the criteria for this "group" discernment must be the search for a common thread of truth. The scriptures encourage this direction. "For it is by wise guidance that you wage your war, and the victory is due to a wealth of counselors" (Prv 24:6). The composition of this discerning group is important. It should be broad enough to give you a good perspective on a particular situation, but not so wide as to cause confusion. Try to avoid seeking advice from someone whose personal life is not in order. You should feel comfortable with their judgment and have confidence that they are reflecting God's truth for you.

When an important decision comes up, pray about it alone then share it with your wife. Anna and I will pray, asking the Lord to build unity between us. If we do not sense any clear guidance from God, I'll discuss the question with my spiritual guide. If together we cannot discern a clear leading of the Spirit, I will then consult a select group of friends to discuss the matter. Following this, I pray again with Anna and make a tentative decision; bringing the composite wisdom of the group back to my principal counselor, along with a tentative decision for his affirmation. All decisions should finally be checked against the word of the Lord.

The criteria for some decisions should be faith in our own common sense and our measure of peace. These inner senses will tell us to do one thing or stop doing something else. I call this "guidance by feel." For me, it's like the chilly feeling I get when I go into an air conditioned room. The sudden change of temperature is analogous to the Spirit saying "Wait! Recheck your path!" This method often works when other types of discernment have produced no clear direction; God will let us know when he wants to guide us directly.

In a blind walk like this, we must rely exclusively on our contact with the Spirit. God calls us into boldness and growth in faith. We need to know his care, even when we have no clear road signs to guide our path. We can only rely on the Father's love and care as we walk one step behind Jesus the Shepherd. "Then, too, heed your own heart's counsel; for what have you that you can depend on more? A man's conscience can tell him his situation better than seven watchmen in a lofty tower. Most important of all, pray to God to set your feet in the path of truth" (Sir 37:13-15).

Abandonment and Personal Freedom

The attitude of submission to Christ leads to abandonment. This is our call to be Christ-like and to put into practice what submission to his will has suggested. God wants his children to reach a point of surrender, where we can say with Charles de Foucauld: "Yes, Jesus is enough. Where he is, nothing is missing."

We probably will not be called to contemplative prayer in the Sahara Desert, but the effects of the gospel on our life and our family can be the same as Brother Charles experienced. We can become free and happy people as we discover that true happiness is possessing the love of Christ. In knowing him we have everything. Like other contradictions to worldly wisdom, total submission to the will of God produces a personal freedom beyond our capacity to comprehend. Thus the foolishness of following Christ in the world draws us into a circle of his love and frees us of our self will.

Thoughts like these didn't come from Bob Iatesta, successful man of the world. They were placed in me by Jesus in slow and steady ways, as he drew me to himself.

My strong individualistic tendencies were clearly manifested in my business relationships. The president of our company, admiring my hunger for success, once said, "Bob, you're difficult to manage, but I'd take one hundred more like you if I could find them." My insecurity drove me in ways unlike other young salesmen, yet it became evident very early in my career that I was not a team player. Our management politely referred to me as "an individual achiever."

I mention this not for confessional value, but to testify that God can work his miracle of abandonment even in the heart of a man who clung to his personal freedom and individuality more than most.

In the gospels, Jesus explained in many ways that our old ways must die in order for rebirth to occur. "I solemnly assure you unless the grain of wheat falls to the earth and dies, it remains just a grain of wheat. But if it dies, it produces much fruit" (Jn 12:24). As the abandonment which God wants proceeds in me, I've come to understand more about that passage. A seed doesn't die instantly when it hits the ground, and neither does the "old man." We die slowly and painfully, but God is in the pain.

The dying process of abandonment has a very important result in a Christian: He eventually becomes *useful* to God in building the Kingdom. We become more able to serve the Lord and our family as we surrender and allow control of our life to slip away. Once our pride is broken, God can forge men who will speak with conviction about Jesus being Lord. Beside my own experience, I have seen this happen to many others. When I see men of abundant natural talents being satisfied to move chairs at a prayer meeting, clean dishes at home, or perform other small, hidden services, I know that the Nazarean carpenter is forging new and strong leaders for his Church. Our humanity is blended with God's Spirit in our personal Nazareth, the quiet place of abandonment and waiting. For some it will happen at home; for others it will happen elsewhere.

Although God clearly calls us to this depth of spiritual perfection, most Christians never reach it. They become fearful and cry for God to stop. So he does. In his book *The Normal Christian Life*, Watchman Nee describes the tragedy of the half-born Christian: "When the Galilean boy brought his bread to the Lord, what did the Lord do with it? He broke it. God will always break what is offered to him. He breaks what he takes, but after breaking it he blesses and uses it to meet the needs of others. After you give yourself to the Lord, he begins to break what was offered to him. Everything seems to go wrong, and you protest and find fault with the ways of God. But to stay there is to be no more than just a broken vessel, no good for the world to use you; and no good for God either because you have not gone far enough for him to use you. You are out of gear with the world, and you have a controversy with God."

We are called to go beyond this state—to a complete conversion. God wants us to go all the way. Our worst pain develops when we try to reverse the process and get things back to safe harbor. My friend Jack Craig summed it up this way: "My problems begin when I start negotiating with God."

A prayer from the pen of Charles de Foucauld opened this chapter. Interestingly enough, this shining witness of submission to Christ never had a single disciple in his lifetime. His life was quiet and almost unnoticed, moved by the gentle breeze of God's Spirit. But just as the wind's power to move the seas is easily missed, so can we fail to comprehend the power of the Spirit to change a man's heart.

We can become discouraged, thinking that our role as a husband and father is an insignificant witness to the Gospel.

When we fall prey to this lie, we become the unfinished Christian described by Watchman Nee. Don't let that happen to the precious seed of faith sown deeply in your heart. Allow God to finish his work in you, by surrendering, abandoning, and becoming free to love.

This is the quiet but life-changing walk of the Christian father who has learned to follow in the footsteps of the Shepherd. He is a man who has become broken enough of pride to submit to the authority which God sets over him. He has allowed the Spirit to curb his personal freedom and conform his will to the Father's.

CHAPTER THIRTEEN

Leading Your Family: Practical Realities

A little while ago, a neighboring couple—the McGuires—questioned Anna and me about authority and spiritual leadership in a family. Art McGuire asked: "Bob, how does it *really* work in your home?" My initial response was to give an analogy of the family as a body, showing spiritual authority as the internal skeleton which brings us into God's order and headship as the external covering of tough muscles and soft skin. I said, "Headship and submission provide a framework for God's love to work within." Then I went on to give some practical examples.

I now realize what a key question Art asked. Therefore, rather than detailing the analogy to describe loving authority, I want to get immediately into the meat of the issue. Today, many men are aware of headship *theoretically*, but their lack of practical experience causes them concern and even fear. Most men know that spiritual authority is needed, but they are timid about admitting a lack of knowledge or experience in exercising it.

I want to emphasize two working principles from my personal experience with Christian headship in the family: initiative and loving communication. Headship is not a cause for insecurity or a tool for domination, but a way of transmitting God's love to a family. It's very practical and it works!

This chapter will contain some concrete examples and suggestions for Christian headship—the personal pastoral care of a family. Before giving them, I want to offer a few words of caution which may avoid unnecessary pain. Our growth into effective headship is a life-long process. By grace, we keep pushing on past our human weakness. An honest look at headship may produce some feelings of frustration or discouragement. These are natural. However, if we linger on negative feelings, they will immobilize us creating confusion and self-condemnation. God wants joy and peace for us, not a constant struggle.

If guilt feelings exist regarding headship, we can ask for God's perspective on our situation. The Father will bless the effort and show us his love. His word will encourage, not condemn us. The Lord wants us to enjoy our family. He will not increase our burden. He said this through Isaiah:

> For I am the Lord, your God
> who grasp your hand;
> It is I who say to you,
> Fear not, I will help you.
> (Is 41:13)

Accept the suggestions this chapter offers with the understanding that they must fit realistically into your own family. Rather than debating the "how to's"—look for practical ways to bring about the main objective of headship: an increase in love.

How Headship Really Works

Headship is God's way of loving a Christian family. It is a channel of grace. The husband and wife both participate in the charism of headship in unique yet complementary ways. Without the cooperation of a holy and loving woman, headship will not produce the results it should. In our home, Anna not only supports my exercise of headship, but she actively participates in it. Much of the direction for our family comes from our consensus and unity. Anna is mainly responsible for the daily workings of our home; she has the unique gifts for it. She also exercises significant spiritual authority in training and forming our children. Authority is even passed on to the older children when we're not available. For example, when the teenagers are babysitting, they participate in headship through obedience to our instructions.

Space will not permit me to discuss everyone's role in a family's experience of spiritual leadership. Therefore, I will focus on only one—the father's. With the understanding that a man cannot function in a vacuum, these pages will deal with the practical aspects of his call as spiritual leader, and loving servant of his family.

Initiative is the first key to any kind of leadership, but it is especially needed in a Christian home. The first initiative is always God's; he is the true leader. When God has taken initiative to touch a man's heart, our response is to imitate that touch by taking initiative with our own family. Spiritual leadership thereby directs a family toward an authentic experience of God.

The exercise of our charism of leadership should produce discernable changes. These usually begin with the father. I'd like to recall a few examples of small changes in my behavior to illustrate the point that headship is something that involves practical realities, not just the spiritual aspects of life in a family. Initiative involves decisions for change.

Not too long ago, I allowed myself to be late quite often. I thought this trait was "just me." While I slept, Anna would have to take the lead in waking the children, helping them dress, feeding them and getting them off to school. Then I would appear so that she could begin to serve me. One morning I got this reading in scripture: "How long, O sluggard, will you rest? When will you rise from your sleep?" (Prv 6:9). That was God speaking to me about change. A word of scripture put the process into motion.

Today things are different. I usually rise first and spend some time in prayer. Then I go to wake up the children, allowing them enough time to rise and prepare themselves for the day. As they are dressing I wake Anna, then go down and prepare the living room for family prayer. Breakfast was set up the night before, so Anna can join us. One of us leads family worship and provides a short teaching on the scriptures. Cooperating with the Lord has led to mornings filled with grace and peace rather than confusion.

Another example of a small but meaningful change occurred after a trip to Ann Arbor. I stayed with the Morgans and watched how Gary entered his home after a day at work. He went straight to his family and ignored any physical disorder. He later admitted to me that this was a big change for him. Gary said he used to arrive home and immediately begin criticizing everyone for not putting things away. Today he spends time with his wife and children first, then pitches in to pick up whatever he can.

I took Gary's example to heart. My behavior was a lot like his had been; complaining as soon as I got home, and expecting perfection from Anna, even though our home was filled with young children and friends most of the time. I also had a habit of looking at the mail or nibbling on a snack before kissing her and the kids. With new awareness and God's help, things have now changed. Today, upon coming home, I go directly to my family. The mail and other things which would draw my attention must wait until I can greet my wife and children. They are my first human priorities.

By exposing my patterns of behavior to God's word and the scrutiny of mature Christian friends, I've learned how much converting I really need. The changes which have occurred in our family have come from God's initiative and my acceptance of his way. They haven't come easily; nothing of lasting value ever does.

These are some basic principles of exercising headship which I have learned as God continues to work with me:
—Set positive examples.
—Seek to love, not to be right.
—Liberate, don't dominate.
—Be available to the needs of the family.
The fifth and sixth chapters of Paul's letter to the Galatians

provide scriptural grounding for these principles of holy initiative. Here are a few verses from those chapters:

A man will reap only what he sows. (6:7)
or
Set positive examples!

It is in the Spirit that we eagerly await the justification we hope for, and only faith can yield it. In Christ Jesus neither circumcision or the lack of it counts for anything; only faith, which expresses itself through love. (5:5-6)
or
Seek to love, not to be right!

It was for liberty that Christ freed us. (5:1)
or
Liberate, don't dominate!

Out of love, place yourself at one another's service. (5:13) Help carry one another's burdens; in that way you will fulfill the law of Christ. (6:2)
or
Be available to the needs of the family!

These attitudes and behavior patterns are cultivated in a unique educational facility. They are the result of special schooling. Let me explain.

The School of the Spirit

I learned about the School of the Spirit from my friend Dom Lettieri. Like me, Dom has been active in Church renewal for many years; his service is now centered in a radio ministry. Also like me, he has little background for his service in the Church, having worked in the garment industry and held a commission in the Air Force. Dom is currently teaching in a local Catholic school. When I told him about my lack of a writing background, he said, "Don't worry brother, God will teach you what you need to know. You will get your degree in the same way I did, from the School of the Spirit!" It is the same with fatherhood and headship—the Holy Spirit is our principal teacher and guide.

The light which shattered the darkness in Nazareth and revealed the truth to the disciples is the same light which guides and teaches us. God has always provided that light for those who are called to lead. As Paul says in the beginning of Galatians: "I assure you, brothers, the gospel I proclaimed to you is no mere human invention. I did not receive it from any man, nor was I schooled in it. It came by revelation from Jesus Christ" (Gal 1:11-12). Paul had received all the knowledge available to a learned Jew of his time, but the light which led him to freedom was sent by Christ, not men.

The Father wants to instruct all of us in a similar way. He wants to send his Spirit to teach us about leading his children. God is committed to our fatherhood.

The lessons in the School of the Spirit are based on our current need for grace. The prerequisite for God's course is something we have mentioned before—surrender. We cannot negotiate with God; we must abandon our total selves, with all our good ideas, to Jesus. When we declare total surrender, he is free to teach us his ways.

Surrender is essential because headship consists largely of leading others into a deeper surrender to Christ. Before we can "call" others effectively, we must have willingly responded to Jesus' call ourselves.

As the Lord's revelation unfolds for your fatherhood, you will be amazed at how positive God is. We are humanly absorbed in our failure, our past, and our sin. By contrast, the Spirit of God calls us into encouragement and affirmation, not condemnation and humiliation. If we spend the time and relinquish our self-will, God can reveal the goodness which he has already placed in us. We needn't fear what God's Spirit will uncover; he already knows us completely and accepts us.

God will not be shocked by a lack of leadership in the family. The pressures of modern life can easily disorient our priorities. Yet we are being called out of past weakness, into the opportunities of today. God is not looking for instant perfection; he wants some raw material, willing to be taught. There are no perfect families or perfect Christian fathers in this life. We all fall short of the fatherhood of God, which is our ideal.

In the School of the Spirit, human failure does not mean expulsion. We are *never* deserted by Christ. Rather, a father learns by his mistakes. They cause us to learn the most important lesson of all: We must continue to surrender to Jesus and rely on his grace instead of resisting it. Scripture has a term for our habitual resistance to God's way. It is called "kicking against the goad" (Acts 26:14). The goad was a harness which was used to hitch up beasts of burden for their task. Saul was kicking against the goad when he was on his way to persecute the Nazarenes in Damascus. God didn't destroy Saul; he stopped him and revealed his plan for Saul's life.

We fathers often find ourselves in this position of non-cooperation with the Lord. When we sense extreme difficulty in carrying out our plan, we should stop and check our direction. When our plans fail and we find ourselves struggling, we should ask, "Lord is this your way?" The next section discusses an area where most men tend to "kick against the goad." It is the heart of headship, and one of the most difficult to exercise in God's way.

Loving Communication

The trinitarian model for a family teaches us that loving dialogue is the natural outgrowth of God's initiative with us. As he lived in the Spirit, Jesus was in steady communication with the Father. As we let the Spirit form us, we learn to communicate our thoughts, our feelings, and our prayer so that a human family is able to develop and maintain the oneness which God wants for it.

Effective communication begins between a husband and wife. This sounds obvious, but I know from experience it cannot be assumed. We are not assured of a relationship or communication just because we live in the same house. Unless we take concrete steps to communicate effectively, the home can easily become only a place where people eat, sleep, and work.

The core of the Christian family is the covenant relationship a husband and wife share with each other and the Lord. In the end, when the kids have grown, the job challenge ebbed, and the social whirlwind subsided, what remains is Jesus and the relationship of a man and woman. This relationship has either grown through regular communication, or it has deteriorated. From our loving interaction in marriage everything else flows.

Anna and I have struggled with regular communication. Here are some ideas which are helping us. Today we:

1. Make explicit decisions about when our communication will take place.
2. Concentrate mainly on affirming each other and balance any negative comments with loving encouragement.
3. Use scripture whenever possible to give more life to our discussions.
4. Pray together in addition to our sharing.

The above principles are applicable to all the communication which goes on in our home. The most important principle is to decide when and how we are going to interact. It does not happen spontaneously. To care for our family, I have had to decide to share with my wife and children on a regular basis. During these times, I have to be fully present and ready to listen to each member of my family. Regular communication is one of the ways headship "really works."

Some examples of the ways we maintain dialogue in our home may illustrate this point and also provide suggestions for your own family. Be free to use your own methods. The important thing is not the method, but rather the decision to communicate in love on a committed basis.

Let's begin with Anna and me. Although we are both outgoing people, it has not been easy to share with each other regularly and effectively. We thought about doing this, but it wasn't until our marriage hit a few rough spots that we decided to schedule out talks together. The decision has borne good fruit in our marriage and family life.

We've divided our communication into two types: functional and personal. Functional communication involves the myriad of decisions which must be made for the daily life of our home. As head of a household, a father should be eager to support his wife in any way he can. Although many of the functional details may be carried out by his wife, the man should still take overall responsibility. This is especially true when a mutual decision has been made to have a woman work outside the home.

Anna and I try to meet every day after dinner to discuss the day's events while the children are doing the dishes. Anna has become a happier woman since I've begun to show a real concern for the details of running a household. It's no longer me and my career, followed by Anna and the kids. Today we work together in our common mission of providing a pleasant place for our family to live. The purpose of this daily time together is to share our day, discuss necessary decisions, and plan ahead. We concentrate on the physical and personal situations which need constant attention.

We also have a regular time when Anna and I share in depth and when I personally care for her. This is an important time for a husband and wife, or any person for that matter, because we all need personal attention. Before church on Sundays, our older children care for the younger ones, allowing us enough freedom to sit quietly together. They know this is a very important time for us, so they don't interrupt unless it's an emergency.

This gives us about an hour of private time together. I will usually ask Anna to share about her personal needs and feelings, her prayer time, her relationship to God, and practical necessities such as adequate rest and quiet time. Sometimes, I am led to affirm her gifts and speak to her as Jesus would, trying to reflect God's mind about her life. She does the same for me. We may pray together or I might simply listen while Anna expresses a hurt or other emotions. Every marriage should have a regular protected period set aside for caring love.

I've come to look forward to these special times when we can sit together with two cups of hot coffee and share deeply about God. Along with the process of growth in the Lord, we open our hearts to the joy and hope which Jesus offers. The goal of these encounters is a sense of being totally present to Jesus and each other, allowing God's love to touch us in an intimate way. That love, shared in Christian marriage, has the power to heal and transform our lives.

With the Lord's help, I am learning how to love Anna in this way. Our experience is convincing me that God wants this depth for all marriages. I don't propose to be an authority on headship, but I believe that if men and women were being shown more personal care and attention, the American family wouldn't be in the shape it's in today.

Obviously a married couple must feel free to speak to each other at any time. But we have found that unless times to discuss functional and spiritual matters are defined, they just will not happen consistently enough and the couple will not develop the solidarity which they need to stay above the inevitable pressures and frustrations of life. The scheduled meetings are essential, yet they are the minimum. We should strive to speak "words of life" to each other at every possible opportunity.

From the loving dialogue between husband and wife flows a channel of grace to our children. We will receive insights into their needs directly from the Lord in prayer, from sharing our daily observations, and from our time alone with them. This last element is one which fathers often neglect. Children love to be singled out for individual attention and they hunger for personal time with us. There is no maximum amount of time for this kind of care. They will gladly receive all we can give.

As I became aware of our children's need for my spiritual guidance and parental care, I was stunned by the enormity of the task. How could I effectively direct six active growing children with varying needs and distinct personalities? The answer came from a good and wise friend, Father Dan Cavanaugh, an experienced counselor and high school teacher. He said, "It's easy Bob. You don't lead all six in the same way. You concentrate your principal attention on the oldest child."

Father Dan explained that each child must pass through a

tunnel of puberty on their way to personal maturity. A major job we have as parents is to guide them through this tunnel. When the oldest child has successfully passed into adolescence and then adulthood, he gives shape to that tunnel for the brothers and sisters who follow him. While focusing special attention on the oldest, we must find a way to insure that the younger ones know they are loved just as much.

This has been our experience: As each young child entered puberty, the good example of the older children has done as much as our personal direction to help them through. This is an example of positive peer pressure right within a natural family. It works, and it takes some pressure off the parents of large families. With this principle in operation, I could relax and direct my greatest effort at personal formation toward Robert, our oldest son. Today my relationship with Rob is fast becoming one of spiritual companionship. However, I am still his father; my care for his life is continued, even though he has navigated the shoals of puberty.

Being an effective father for our children required meeting with them regularly, much as I do with Anna. The need for regular sharing seems to intensify as the children go into their teens. In fact, the greatest test of fatherhood is effective direction for adolescents. Young children have relatively simple needs, but the demand for emotional and spiritual direction is the greatest in the teen years. Consequently, this age is when the father's headship must be operating in high gear. Both challenges and opportunities abound. Raising adolescents successfully can provide our best witness to a confused world struggling with a teenage counter-culture. By providing a better answer in Christ, we show the world how powerful the gospel message is.

My weekly time with our adolescents centers on their prayer lives, spiritual and school study programs, personal relationships, and social activities. These are not necessarily corrective sessions, but concentrate mostly on affirmation and encouragement. A young person needs to receive praise and be called on to grow in Christ. I also ask the children to offer suggestions about our home and how we can better support their lives. This time is spent to build a foundation of love and relationship, which is necessary if we are to deal effectively with the correction that will invariably be needed at other times.

Fathers build a relationship of headship with their children in various ways. Some will write out an explicit schedule for sharing; others will rely on the grace of the moment. My advice is to avoid extremes: Be flexible enough to adapt to changing conditions, yet consistent enough to keep circumstances and pressures from controlling your time together. It's a good idea to work around your natural family patterns to avoid making individual headship become a heavy burden. None of us have "spare time," but everyone has little blocks in our schedule which are flexible enough to be refocused toward our priorities.

My good friend, Pete Radice, a father of five, seems to have achieved this balance. Each night after dinner, the family unwinds and spends time together. After finishing their meal and friendly conversation, they have a time for family prayer and scripture reading. Following this, one child spends time with Pete for ten to fifteen minutes while the others clean up the dishes. The entire time—meal, family prayer, personal sharing, cleanup, and sometimes an activity—takes less than an hour and a half. What an investment of ninety minutes!

Fathers can use other means to spend personal time with their children. Some take a child for a walk after dinner or before bed; some talk while they work or play together; others take short trips. The method isn't critical, but it must accomplish the end—a fruitful relationship with your children. Use whatever style fits your situation, taking advantage of what comes naturally.

What about Anna? How does she fit into the exercise of pastoral care? Although her role is more subtle, a mother plays a critical part in headship over the children. My wife talks with our children more than I do, and has more opportunity to listen to them. Her insights give my headship its principal direction. There is something special in a mother's love which a man can admire but not imitate. Men and women are different and the children know it. They also know that in Jesus we're united, so they don't try to manipulate us or play favorites (at least not too often).

In addition to impromptu listening, Anna takes an active role in headship in two other ways. Each week she takes one child to early mass and breakfast out. The kids eagerly await this treat—their special time with Mom. She also participates in straightening out those difficult, complex or serious situations that all children get into. When a tough problem comes up, Anna and I initially discuss it, then usually bring in the child to confront it together. This "two-on-one" approach is very effective since it gives us an advantage of wisdom, grace, and plain endurance. The deeper the problem, the longer these sessions take. But once begun, they take a priority over other activities.

On one occasion we discovered one of our children had lied to us to cover up some friends in school. In our home, lying is a serious offense, along with overt rebellion, disobedience, and hurting others. The child had gone to bed, but Anna and I decided to awaken her and confront her in love and truth. That session lasted from 11 p.m. to 2 a.m., but it ended well. One of us could never have sustained that situation alone; together we were able to persevere in truth to victory. Serious sin and wrongdoing doesn't go away; it eats away at a child's spirit. It must be rooted out and confessed, regardless of the cost.

As children move through adolescence into adulthood, the focus of our leadership for their lives will change. Rob, our oldest, is approaching graduation from high school. I'm seeing that I must now guide him in life directions and career choices. He needs me for understanding and wisdom as he struggles with the pull of the world and the call of Jesus. I try to encourage him to keep his eyes on the Lord, investing the time necessary to help him sort out his direction in life.

God's plan is to direct his children toward some work which will bring them joy (Eccl 3:22). I told our son this, assuring him that my deepest desire is to see him happy and submitting to God's plan for his life. I've also told Rob that I will always stand beside him and that he will never have to face an important decision alone. He recently told me the assurance of that kind of support has lifted the pressure he was experiencing, and has provided the peace he needs to listen to the Lord. I think these words of Thomas Merton's summed up his feelings: "Dear God, I have no idea where I'm going. I do not see the road ahead of me. I will trust you always. I know you will never leave me to face my decisions alone."

What To Expect

Loving authority is a gift from God to a family, yet a man's exercise of headship can produce both positive and negative reactions. It helps to anticipate some of the negative reactions which may follow increased efforts at Christian headship.

The first is a natural rebellion which is woven into our damaged human fabric. The Evil Spirit, exerting an influence on all of us, will vigorously resist any force which would tend to produce freedom and order in the Kingdom of God. Our deep instincts of pride and stubborness will probably assert themselves when authority is called for.

We can expect some rebellion in both our family and ourself as we grow in headship. But don't be confused by these negative reactions. They are only temporary. The fruit of loving authority will very quickly show them for what they are: mere feelings, not objective reasons to return to our old ways. In essence, they are withdrawal symptoms, not much different than the craving for sugar an overweight person will feel when he tries to diet. As in prayer, the fruit of headship comes as we push past our human weakness.

Along with the reaction of rebelliousness, we can expect normal uneasiness and confusion which accompanies a change in any area of life. Some confused looks and negative comments may come out simply because we are doing something different. When I first asked to have a personal session with our 10-year-old son John, he looked at me sheepishly and said, "What have I done wrong now Dad?" That reaction showed me that many times in the past I had spoken to him personally just to correct him.

The positive reactions a father can expect are signs of evident, beneficial change. Once the shock of having a spiritual leader at home wears off and the natural rebellion is challenged and overcome, headship will produce good fruit. In our home, a distinct peace and a new sense of physical order have developed. These were external signs that something in our hearts was being changed for the good.

We noticed other changes beside physical order and a sense of peace. My wife and children began to seek my guidance and companionship. As our love grew, so did a desire to be together. Effective headship has provided an environment for God's love to flourish.

These are not dreams, but reality. They are the blessings a man of God should expect. You can expect them too.

We will discuss how to begin assuming spiritual authority in more detail in the next chapter. For now, if your headship has been lacking, may I suggest beginning to exercise it *as soon as possible*. Keep it light at first until a base of trust is built. Trust will grow as we demonstrate a desire to love unconditionally. This isn't easy, but God is on our side and he will get us through. "Cast your care upon the Lord, and he will support you; never will he permit the just man to be disturbed" (Ps 55:23).

As a final word, I'd like to offer a note of caution to men who feel they already "have it together." You will tend to relax in the exercise of your headship. Fight that tendency! Expect to be attacked by Satan, since the flow of God's love into a family will starve his agents. "Stay sober and alert. Your opponent the devil is prowling like a roaring lion looking for someone to devour. Resist him, solid in your faith, realizing that the brotherhood of believers is undergoing the same sufferings throughout the world" (1 Pt 5:8-9).

Remain humble before God, always conscious of human weakness. Beware of overconfidence and complacency. There is no end to the growth God can work in a man's heart. No matter how far we've already come, the Lord wants to continue his work of renewal and restoration in us and those whom we serve.

St. Paul described the Christian as a person engaged in a battle and needing the full armor of God to persevere. He is exactly right; the battle is real and the stakes are very high. We are fighting for life and the freedom to love. Christian headship is God's armor to insure the safe passage of his children through an alien land loaded with dangers. It is combat leadership! During a battle we have little choice but to take the initiative, make decisions, and act boldly.

The major offensive weapon given to a father is the gift of encouragement. As he affirms his family and calls it on, the battle is won. In addition to offensive action to take new territory, the father receives the defense of grace to secure those situations already won for the King.

Thomas a Kempis' *Imitation of Christ* offers these prophetic words, "Fight like a good soldier; and if sometimes you fall through frailty, rise up again with greater strength than before, trusting in my abundant grace; but guard yourself against self-confidence and pride. Through these many are led into error and sometimes fall into a blindness well nigh incurable. Let this humbling of the proud, who foolishly rely on their own strength, serve you as a warning and keep you always aware of your own capabilities."

CHAPTER FOURTEEN

Taking Your Place as a Father

A few years ago Anna and I were having dinner at a restaurant with our friends Romolo and Lorraine Leone. We had ordered a meal that promised to be delicious and we couldn't wait for it to be served. While sipping wine and chatting about what God was doing in our lives, Romolo became strangely silent. Four piping hot dishes were set before us, but instead of picking up his fork and knife, Romolo asked for a pencil and paper. There at the table, while our meal was served, Romolo wrote down a prophecy. Prophecy is a spiritual gift which the Lord often gives when he baptizes someone in the Spirit. It is a way the Spirit can exhort and direct us. "The prophet speaks to men for their upbuilding, their encouragement, their consolation" (1 Cor 14:3). This is the prophecy Romolo handed me that night at dinner:

I do not want you to act with a timid spirit. I have raised you up to be a son of mine and I want to move and act through you.

I want you to act in boldness. Do not look at the circumstances around you anymore. Do you not realize who I am and what power I have? I want you to come to me and seek me for the answers you want. I want you to put your whole trust in me.

I have a vision for you that you can not comprehend. The way in which I work you will sometimes not understand; but it is not for you to have the understanding now. When I call you to do something, I want you to do it. Move when I tell you to move. Stop when I tell you to stop.

I now want you and Anna to give up your anxiety for the children I've given you. I will heal in them what you've been having fears for.

When Satan attacks you, do not believe I have left you. Know I am with you and have a very special love for you both. To show my love for you, I am going to give an experience of my love in a very special way. I don't want you to anticipate my blessings for you, but to receive the grace I give you each day and know full well, I am with you and will never leave you.

I believe these words are for all Christian fathers, not just for me. They should stir our hearts and affirm the sacramental grace we have received. God is calling us to boldness and radical trust in him.

The Lord confirmed the prophecy as he promised by beginning to heal the heart trouble of my father-in-law, Dan DiBona. A few weeks after our night out with the Leones, Dad attended a healing service. In the months that followed, he experienced physical healing as well as deeper spiritual renewal in the family.

Although the Lord had spoken very clearly, I continued to experience resistance within myself. God was calling for boldness, but I didn't *feel* very bold. My response to God's call developed slowly. It progressed on the basis of grace and my decision to be obedient. I had to go beyond my feelings. The result has been an ongoing change in my attitudes and behavior. Knowing the struggle and the fear involved in overcoming our old ways, I want to encourage all fathers to keep moving. Change isn't easy for any of us; but the power of God's love is greater than our timidity. His promise is sure.

God wants loving authority flowing into Christian homes.

He is calling fathers to become effective leaders, to accept and use grace he has already provided. God wants changed hearts and restored families. He is offering us a fresh start.

Affirming Ourselves

Success in our fatherhood can be very difficult to measure because there are few objective criteria. Our temptation is to use human and worldly standards to determine how well we are responding to the call of the Lord. This can cause us to become excessively self-critical and judgmental. Thus, as we become bolder fathers, it is important to look at ourselves through God's perspective.

Although we might try to appropriate the full power of our fatherhood in a quick burst of holiness, we soon discover that God's ways are slower and more practical. He wants perseverence! To persevere I keep one idea before me all the time: "I am the *perfect* father for my family." This is God's perspective. It's positive. It would make a good banner to hang on your bathroom mirror, so you can receive the Lord's truth each morning.

The Word of the Lord continues to affirm his call to us: "Fear not, for I have redeemed you; I have called you by name: you are mine. When you pass through the water, I will be with you; in the rivers you shall not drown. When you walk through fire, you shall not be burned; the flames shall not consume you" (Is 43:1, 2). As fathers, we can fulfill God's call to, "Bring back my sons from afar, and my daughters from the ends of the earth" (Is 43:6). Believe this, with a bold and active faith, for it is the truth. We are the men whom God has chosen to lead and care for our families. We can't assign a substitute.

Our faith in God's goodness extends to our whole family. Mark's story of the possessed boy is the classic lesson to men about the protection extended to their families through faith in their fatherhood. The disciples had been unable to deliver this child from the grip of an evil spirit. Jesus then looked to the boy's father who begged, "'If out of the kindness of your heart you can do anything to help us, please do!' Jesus said, 'If I can?

Everything is possible for a man who trusts.' The boy's father exclaimed, 'I do believe! Help my lack of trust'" (Mk 9:22-24).

That father exercised a weak and stumbling faith, but it was enough to release God's power to free his child. We have access to the same strength and protection if we will only call on the Spirit to teach us to trust and believe.

Our personal relationship with Jesus is the key to our fatherhood. The faith to believe and to act on our belief comes from a steady remembrance of our encounter with him. We must remind ourselves that we *have* and *are* rejecting Satan and that we *did* and *still do* accept Jesus as our personal Lord and Savior. Through Jesus, we are sons of God and heirs to the treasures of the Father.

I evangelize myself in words like these every morning, as my feet slip out of bed and before I take my first step of that day. The good news that I am the "beloved" of God should be ever before me. It is important to remember—as soon as my conscious mind opens to new thoughts—where my allegiance lies. Sensing strong temptation during the day, I repeat the truth of who I am and what I believe. This prepares my heart to praise God, rejoicing in my sonship. Thoughts like these bring forth the grace to trust again and to move on.

Affirming ourselves in this way is not merely positive thinking. It is our personal good news. Jesus has saved us, and his Spirit living within empowers us to know, love, and serve God. Our minds need to be reshaped daily into the mind of Christ. A Christian father who thinks and speaks affirmatively is a man who brings life to his family and himself. He is God's herald in the midst of a world crying for hope. "How beautiful upon the mountains are the feet of him who brings glad tidings, announcing peace, bearing good news, announcing salvation, and saying to Zion, 'Your God is King!'" (Is 52:7).

A Shepherd's Heart

As God's word stirs us, we are drawn deeper into relationship with him. Our part in this process is to ask the Spirit to complete his work. "Ask and you will receive." Ask for a hunger to pursue the call to shepherd your family.

What is a shepherd's heart? What are some of the qualities a shepherd needs? What are the qualities we should ask for and expect to receive?

Jesus is calling each of us to become bold yet gentle men. These words seem almost contradictory, but they work together. We are to act boldly, yet love tenderly. The headship of Christ, drawing a father into the fullness of his manhood, brings about this blending of the human and divine nature. It takes a strength beyond ourselves to exercise authority in love; to be strong, yet tender. God must bring this about in us; we can't do it alone.

A shepherd's heart is a listening heart. It is in constant touch with Jesus and the Father through the Holy Spirit. As we exchange our ways for God's, we become more interested in doing his will than in realizing our own ideas. That means we spend time listening to the Chief Shepherd for his plan in caring for our portion of the flock. The voice of Jesus becomes clear; over the din of our desires, we hear the gentle, persistent call to love.

The shepherd's heart is attuned to the purposes of God. The Lord needs men who will listen and act, even when their human wisdom speaks caution.

Imagine how Joseph felt when an angel appeared to him with a command. "Get up, take the child and his mother and flee to Eygpt. Stay there until I tell you otherwise" (Mt 2:13). For the first few days, Joseph probably had the vivid memory of that dream in his mind, but what about the days that followed? God didn't send an angel every night. He expected this man to receive his command and carry it out without constant reinforcement.

Like Joseph, we have to move and stop at God's direction. Our heart must become so eager to do God's work that the voice of Jesus can set our direction, despite the distractions of our modern Egypt. The journey back to the Father is one of faith. We may have vivid experiences of him, but we do not expect them as our requirement for obedience. The cost of love is our daily "yes" to the gentle voice of the Lord inviting us to

"Come follow me." We follow in love, not our love, but his, given freely to those who respond to God's call to gather and tend his flock.

A shepherd's heart is persistent and always wakeful. The shepherd is constantly aware of the movements of those in his care, pointing them in the right direction when they stray. The flock must be kept moving in order to remain healthy; there is no time when the shepherd can relax his concern for their well-being. A father perseveres in selfless service.

At the end of each day, as shepherds of God's flock, we should ask: "Am I at peace with God? Have I been obedient to his Spirit today?" The grace to redirect ourselves toward Jesus is always available to us, through his divine mercy.

We can rely on the power of God to bring these things about. We are the clay pots which the Spirit is firing into vessels of sacrifice and strength. We are men in the process of being remade into shepherds after his own heart.

Adjusting to Change

Ongoing conversion is a miracle which God somehow manages to work in a man's heart. A father must change to give his family a fresh start, yet those who live with him also experience change. His wife and children must now adjust to new behavior.

I know from first-hand experience that this adjustment can be painful. It is usually most painful for the wife of a new zealot.

For years I worked on Cursillo weekends. For years we would caution men who were newly on fire with God's love to return home carefully, to realize that while they've changed, everyone else at home is the same. Our advice was often ignored. Men would return home, announce a completely new approach, and immediately try to implement it. This usually disoriented their wives. Sometimes the confusion of women who had been praying for their husbands for years was sad to behold. Those prayers were answered, but often not in the way wives had expected. Many times the tension this caused was so severe that healing of the marriage took quite a while.

This happens because there has been a significant shift in behavior. The balance of spiritual authority, which may have previously rested in the women's hands, was now moving into proper balance. This is a substantial change, and it produces a substantial need for adjustment on her part.

Unfortunately, in many cases, mother is shepherding the family in American homes today. That's not the way God intended it, but it's a common condition. I know, because my own home fell into that category for many years. In many Christian homes, the wife is struggling alone under the demands of spiritual leadership.

Fathers, receive this word of caution in love: God wants us to grow in headship, but he doesn't want our wives maimed in the process. As we accept grace to become effective fathers, our wives may perceive the change as "bad times" unless we are careful. Our call is to love, not force her through changes. The ways of God are patient, gentle, and enduring. If she severly resists a vigorous effort to fulfill this aspect of being a father, take that as a sign to *go easy*. Our first call is for unity in marriage. Without that, the power of God cannot be properly channeled into our homes.

From my personal experience, I can assure you that resistance to headship will subside as trust grows and love becomes generous. Love generously. Your wife has probably been doing this for quite a while. In just about every case I can remember, the wife was ultimately able to release the bondage of misplaced authority and do so with joy. God has placed in her heart a desire to have her husband's strength and protection covering her, but she must grow in trust to allow that to happen. Our fidelity to God's call enables her trust to grow.

Submission of a woman to a man follows the same pattern as the man's submission to Christ. He draws submission gently out of us; we must do the same for those we lead. I exhort and encourage you to make a peaceful transformation in this area. Trust that: "Love never fails" (1 Cor 13:8).

Any change, even for the good, should be expected to produce a reaction in those surrounding it. The birth of a child is a perfect example. Although the change is miraculous, each person interacting with that child must accept a revision in their way of life. The entire family feels the effect. Eventually, an acceptance develops and the gift can be seen as wonderful. But growing into that awareness is not always easy.

I might suggest approaching growth in loving authority as a significant change and applying the steps suggested at the end of the first chapter of this book:

—Approach those you love prayerfully and honestly.

—Listen for God's way. Avoid confusion by setting attainable goals, like short periods of regular sharing or prayer together.

—Expect God, who initiates all change for the good, to fill your need for wisdom and grace, in responding to his call.

—Accept and trust that the Spirit will meet you wherever you are and lead the way.

—Expect God to do what you can't.

Believing that you are a son of God, expect that an increase in your capacity to love is central to the heart of the Father. "There are in the end three things that last: faith, hope and love, and the greatest of these is love" (1 Cor 13:13).

The greatest hope of Christianity is the opportunity to begin again, looking forward with Jesus and not backward to condemnation. In this spirit of hope, the Lord calls each of us on. Regardless of past success or failure at fathering, God promises more blessing for the future. We can appropriate his grace in deeper ways each day as we move from one challenge to the next.

The call to grow in fatherhood may mean that some must begin. For others, it means a recommitment to things we've known yet somehow have been unable to put into practice. In either case, decide to push on to finish the race. The power we need can only come from God. In closing I'd like to offer you this "prayer for empowering":

Father, you are the source of life and love. I rejoice in the sonship you offer me, accepting all that my relationship with you implies. For those times when I have doubted or mistrusted your love, please forgive me.

Jesus, my brother and my shepherd—pray with me, walk with me, lead me home. I want to be formed into a man of faith, in your image and based on your gospel. Some day, I want to hear you say, "Father, here is my friend."

Spirit of love, you are the deepest reality in my life. You bring the power of love, as a burning flame in my heart. You light my path to eternity.

God of Power, release in me and my brothers, the faith, hope, and love you offer. Working with our human weakness, build us into men who can call others beyond themselves. Let your power weld us into bonds of unity we call "family." May your life in us come alive and make a difference in our world.

Index